Not Jealous

NOT JEALOUS

Overcoming The Spirit And Emotion Of Jealousy

SEETSE MASIGO

Not Jealous

Published under So Sought Out
ISBN: 978-0-7961-8677-5 (Print)

Author: Seetse Masigo
Contacts:083 563 7045| seetsek@gmail.com

This book was produced with the assistance of
Bono Lashu Publishers
Contacts: publish@bonolashu.co.za | 072 221 9708

Book Cover Credits: Seetse Masigo

CONTENTS

PART THREE

PART FOUR

PART FIVE

PART SIX

ACKNOWLEDGEMENTS

I would like to extend my heartfelt appreciation to the Holy Trinity, Father, Son, and Holy Spirit, for their invaluable guidance, strength, wisdom, and truth. The insights presented in these pages have unfolded beautifully, inspired by the Holy Spirit, making the journey through uncertainty feel much more manageable.

To my husband, thank you for standing with me through every high and every low. Your steadfast love and quiet confidence carried me forward on days when I doubted myself, and your joy in my success reminds me that I never walk alone. Your encouragement, both in words and in your loyal presence, has been my firm foundation. I pray that God's richest blessings overflow in your life

A special thank you to Tebogo Nchoe and Buyisiwe Dladla for your thoughtful feedback, and to Kulani Zitha your contributions have been immensely valuable. Many thanks to everyone who contributed to the survey by sharing their experiences of jealousy. Your honesty gave this work real depth and meaning.

And to you, the reader, who holds this book in your hands: may you discover here not only insight and encouragement but also a path to break free from the grips of jealousy, finding instead the peace and purpose God has for you.

Finally, to my family, each of you has shaped my life in unique ways. I know support can look different from one person to the next, and I honour the love you have shown me in all its forms. Your presence in my life is a gift I cherish.

This book benefited greatly from the insights of pastors, theologians, Bible scholars, who generously shared their wisdom. Your teachings have been instrumental in helping me understand and articulate this message.

Thank you.

Seetse Masigo

PREFACE

Every journey begins with a thoughtful question, and for me, it was both straightforward and transformative: Who am I, and what is my true purpose? I have desired to follow the calling God has placed on my life, that is to serve with sincerity, uphold integrity, embody God's love, build genuine connections, and find my rightful place within ba dumedi (the community of believers).

I have gone through many forms of rejection over time, a common experience, I suspect, many encounter. I would notice something alarming: those I anticipated would support me seemed less available. I sensed the impact of unspoken contrasts from a distance. It became apparent that I was experiencing the effects of jealousy directed towards me. During these times of relational strain, a recurring thought was jealousy. It manifested as gentle resistance or took on various forms. I became keenly interested in this emotion and began noticing it across different environments and dynamics.

I observed its presence in various settings, including churches, families, communities, and friendships. Over time, I recognised that jealousy could go beyond a mere emotion; it can evolve into a hidden force that disrupts the unity that God desires for people.

It falsifies our reality, promotes seeds of doubt, and subtly reduces our peace. This understanding inspired me to write this book.

"Not Jealous" weaves together personal reflections with insights from psychology and theology. It presents reflections, scripture passages, practical tools, and authentic stories for consideration and reflection.

I hope that as you engage with this text, you will find it relevant, deepen your understanding of the impact of jealousy, and uncover paths to healing. Whether you have faced jealousy firsthand, been affected by someone else's envy, or found yourself the target of jealousy, I encourage you to reflect on these insights.

PROLOGUE

Imagine a time when a community walked freely in God's purpose with no urge to compete, and every person knew their unique assignment. In those days, everyone pressed on with confidence, certain that their contribution mattered and that they were accepted just as they were. But over the years, subtle questions crept in: "Why them instead of me?" Soon, eyes drifted from one neighbor's progress to another's, and a hunger for external praise drowned out steady dedication. The spark of unity dimmed whenever someone was recognised; heartfelt praise turned lukewarm, and conversations grew tense.

Amid the unrest, one person refused to follow the trend. They showed up, day after day, trusting God's timing and focusing on their journey. Their unwavering commitment reminded everyone that celebrating another's success never steals our worth. Slowly, the community began to remember what it had lost. By letting go of jealousy and encouraging one another, they rediscovered the simple joy of walking side by side in God's calling.

Here, too, you will learn how to reclaim that freedom: to stand firm in your purpose, support others without envy, and shine together with shared purpose and mutual encouragement.

INTRODUCTION

On a warm Sunday, gathered beneath the gentle shade of the White Stinkwood, a family came together for their annual "stokvel," a traditional South African savings club where members contribute a fixed amount of money to a central fund regularly. Plates of pap, braai meat, and chakalaka were passed hand to hand, and laughter floated in the air. Yet, beneath this easy warmth, fleeting glances passed between cousins, and smiles faded before they fully formed.

"Where envy and self-seeking exist, confusion and every evil thing are there."
—James 3:16, NKJV

The tension centered on one relative who, earlier that week, had announced a recent promotion, the lead role in a multimillion-rand project, and the celebration of another milestone. These clear signs of success felt like an unspoken challenge. Envy crept in like shadows, turning a familiar celebration into a silent contest. These small ruptures, such as a colleague being left out of planning meetings or maybe the respectful "congratulations" that sting, are not dramatic confrontations, but rather relatively soft bruises.

The nod of respect, the invitation to collaborate, and the unguarded word of encouragement all carry weight. When these everyday courtesies vanish, a quiet tension takes hold; conversations become forced, eyes avoid each other, and compliments suddenly bear hidden meanings.

Such silent rivalry, often unnoticed, can be one of the most subtle and agonizing forms of hurt, inflicted by those closest to us, family members, old and current friends alike, coworkers, and people once trusted. Because it masquerades as courtesy or harmless restraint, it often goes unnamed and unchallenged.

You are not alone in this situation; silent rivalry is more common than we might think. These unspoken tensions can alter our self-image and damage our relationships. They can replace joy with worry and unity with suspicion, weakening the trust that holds people together.

This book is divided into five parts:

Part 1: Foundations of Jealousy

Learn to spot the subtle signs, such as guarded smiles, awkward silences, and inner unease, so you can identify when jealousy is a persistent issue and begin addressing its root cause.

Part 2: Community and Culture - Cultural and Relational Contexts

Discover how unspoken expectations in families, workplaces, and faith communities feed competition and rivalry, and find practical ways to foster genuine support instead.

Part 3: Personal and Relational Wounds

See how jealousy fractures our closest bonds among friends, families, siblings, coworkers, and gain clear strategies to speak honestly, rebuild trust, and celebrate others without shrinking back.

Part 4: Exposing Jealousy's Deceptive Cloak

Uncover the hidden alliances and contracts that allow jealousy to take root, learn to discern its counterfeit "spiritual" voice, and arm yourself with God's truth to dismantle the lies that stir suspicion and division.

Part 5: Freedom and Restoration

Walk step by step through deliverance prayers, break generational patterns of envy, close the doors of jealousy that have been opened, and adopt practical, ongoing habits that secure lasting peace.

Envy Vs. Jealousy

A Clarifying Note

Have you ever noticed a teammate's forced smile as you enter a meeting, or a friend's sudden change of subject when your name comes up? These moments, while seemingly similar, originate from two noticeably different emotions: envy and jealousy. While people often use these terms interchangeably, understanding their distinction and how they relate is crucial. Understanding this is what enables us to deal with the underlying effects jealousy can have.

Envy promotes internal battles. It pushes you outward, directing your attention to someone else's accomplishments, relationships, or possessions, making you focus on what you wish you had. This restless focus can either inspire personal growth, a desire to develop new skills, or lead to bitterness and resentment toward others' achievements.

Jealousy, on the other hand, is a destructive force that arises from a fear of losing something you already possess. It occurs in situations like close collaboration, where you suddenly notice a co-worker involving someone new in your project and worry that your contributions will be lessened. It can happen in a longstanding friendship when your friend begins confiding more in another person, making you anxious about losing your importance.

In a ministry team or volunteer group, jealousy may surface when new members arrive, and you fear that your role or voice will be overshadowed.

People often blur the lines between *"jealousy"* and *"envy"* in casual conversation. When someone says, *"I'm jealous of her career,"* they might mean they are envious of her success.

However, true jealousy involves a deeper fear, like worrying that someone will take your place or attention from someone important to you. This discussion focuses on that complex emotion of jealousy and how it can damage relationships and self-esteem.

This is not a textbook on clinical psychology; you won't find diagnostic categories or case studies within its pages. Instead, you will encounter clear, faith-based reflections and real-world examples that illustrate the tactics of jealousy: the sudden silence at a dinner table, the hesitant compliment in a group setting, the shift in seating arrangements at meetings. These faith-based reflections will reassure you that you're not alone in your struggle with jealousy.

Scriptural stories, such as Cain's suspicion of Abel, highlight jealousy as a force that, if ignored, can be dangerous.

As you move forward, you'll learn to identify specific behaviours that indicate jealousy in various aspects of life: at work, in family life, among friends, within community or volunteer groups, in ministry teams, in romantic relationships, and even in extended or online networks.

You'll explore practical, step-by-step strategies grounded in honesty, renewed perspective, and a commitment to truth that'll help you confront the fear of displacement, rebuild authentic connections, and support others' successes without defensiveness.

These strategies will empower you to overcome jealousy, allowing you to stand securely in your calling and celebrate others wholeheartedly.

Envy And Jealousy

Why They Often Feel The Same

At first glance, envy and jealousy might seem like two sides of the same coin, but they have distinct underlying emotions. Envy is the feeling of wanting something someone else has, while jealousy is the fear of losing something you already possess. Both emotions stem from insecurity and feelings of inadequacy.

For example, when a friend gets a promotion, it's natural to feel happy for them, but if a knot forms in your chest, it might be more than just happiness. If you're worried that their success will change how they treat you or how others perceive you, that's jealousy. It's the fear of being left behind or losing your place in the relationship. On the other hand, if you're feeling envious, you might wish you had their success or opportunities.

Understanding the difference between these emotions can help you navigate complex feelings and relationships. By recognising whether you're feeling envious or jealous, you can address the root cause of your emotions and respond in a more thoughtful way. Over time, this fear can result in changes in behaviour.

You might avoid openly celebrating, hesitate in praising them, or begin to question their motives in discussions that previously flowed easily. Suddenly, you build a wall of suspicion where trust once existed.

These changes in behaviour cannot only strain your relationships but also take a toll on your mental and emotional health, leading to increased stress and anxiety. Recognising and managing these emotions is therefore crucial for your overall well-being.

Psychologists and philosophers have long recognised the ease of confusing these two emotions. In biblical Greek and Latin, a single word describes both concepts. Scripture often mentions them together, warning that wherever envy or jealousy take root, *"confusion and every evil practice"* follow.

However, distinguishing between them is essential. Both emotions can strain relationships, but they require different responses. Envy invites us to cultivate gratitude for our journeys, while jealousy urges us to trust that God's blessings are abundant and not limited. Understanding and managing these emotions can empower us to navigate our relationships with more emotional intelligence and control.

Initially, you might endure a sense of being excluded from the joy and accomplishments that others are showcasing, feeling as though you're on the outside looking in.

The pain of envy often comes from more than just missing out on something. It's about feeling like you were never meant to have it in the first place. This feeling is difficult to articulate. It's not about a specific loss or missed opportunity; it's about a deep-seated belief that certain things, like being celebrated, are not within your reach.

You may have never been the first choice, received praise without effort, or felt truly accepted without having to prove your worth. Over time, this absence can alter your self-perception. When you witness someone else's success, it's not just about desiring what they have or missing out on the celebrations. It triggers a thoughtful questioning of your own identity. You don't just feel left out; you feel like you don't belong in the circle of people who witness such moments. You might start to believe that happiness and success are reserved for others, while your life feels like a perpetual state of waiting or being missed.

This is where envy turns into something heavier. It's not really about the car or the post; it's about wondering if you will ever be seen in the same way. It's about fearing that your name was missed when opportunities for love or success were given out.

That fear hurts. It shapes how you pray, dream, and view God. It can make you question whether you are worthy of His love and blessings. It can be challenging to accept blessings because you may feel undeserving or that you were not meant to receive them. This is the deeper issue beneath the surface that makes feeling at peace seem so far away, even when you're not competing openly with anyone.

If left unexamined, envy can become jealousy, leading you to guard your own heart or resist another person's success without realising it.

To heal both emotions, we need to look beyond the surface. It is insufficient to label them; we must confront the questions they raise: *"What do I believe about myself when I desire that promotion?"* and *"What do I fear losing when I see someone celebrated?"* Jesus invites us to replace worry with trust, reminding us that our worth does not depend on others' achievements.

NOT JEALOUS

Overcoming The Spirit And Emotion Of Jealousy

PART ONE: THE FOUNDATION

Recognising The Subtle Rise Of Jealousy

Before we can confront the emotional, relational, and spiritual toll of jealousy, we must first define its essence. Jealousy is a quiet intruder, a subtle whisper on the breeze that unexpectedly chills the warmth and companionship between friends. This emotion often slips in during moments meant for celebration. Instead of filling the air with joy and shared enthusiasm, jealousy casts a shadow, creating an uncomfortable tension that contrasts sharply with the happiness that should have enveloped the moment. Imagine sharing a hard-won breakthrough or a long-answered prayer: the room ought to vibrate with joy, yet you notice smiles flattening and compliments growing dull.

In that moment, you feel the chill of jealousy as conversations lose their sparkle, and genuine enthusiasm is replaced by a sense of distance. This invasion strikes hardest in our closest circles, among family members, in small groups, within ministry teams, and among lifelong friends, where trust is assumed and vulnerability is highest. When one person's light shines a little brighter, those around them may lean back instead of forward. At that moment changes in someone's tone or a quick glance can show signs of jealousy.

Jealousy often unfolds in a predictable pattern. It starts with a trigger, like someone else's achievement or recognition, followed by a shift from genuine approval to awkward manners or silence. Ultimately, behaviour changes, leading to strained relationships and unspoken competition. Imagine the campfire flames dancing together under the stars, when one flame jumps higher, the others shrink back, fearing their light will be diminished. This is often how jealousy works - it can make us want to hide our talents or hold back, thinking that by doing so, we're protecting others or maintaining harmony. However, this can ultimately harm our relationships and community. The example of Jesus is a powerful reminder that God's blessings are abundant and meant to be shared freely. He didn't let the potential for envy or opposition stop Him from performing miracles or speaking truth. Instead, He shone brightly, offering love and light to all, and inviting others to do the same. True freedom from jealousy begins with self-awareness. We start to notice how jealousy manifests in us, how our thoughts shift, differences creep in, and how hard it becomes to celebrate others genuinely. However, we also learn to pay attention when we are on the receiving end, when a friend's voice flattens, when their praise feels hesitant, or when their support quietly fades. In both cases, freedom comes when we stop tying our worth to anyone else's reaction. Instead, we begin to stand secure in who we are, no longer shaped by similarities or silence, but by confidence in God's view of us.

When Jealousy Finds a Seat at the Table

Jealousy, a master of disguise, often lurks behind calm reactions, rather than loud arguments. It cautiously infiltrates where connections once thrived. In workplaces, colleagues who once sought your input now subtly exclude your name from meeting invitations or question your ideas with unexpected care.

Within families, it can develop when a parent lavishes praise on one child while responding to the other's accomplishments with a gentle, *"That's nice,"* as if praising either one too much would disturb an unspoken balance. In some church settings, the same people who once supported you and celebrated your calling may start to hold back. What used to be open support now feels cautious, as if your growth makes them uneasy. It can feel like they are hesitant, not because you've changed, but because your rising influence stirs up their own insecurity or fear of being ignored. Instead of cheering you on, they seem worried that encouraging you too much might take away something from them, like attention, control, or their status. In personal relationships, it can be a friend who suddenly becomes distant when you share good news, or a partner who appears less supportive when you reach a personal goal.

Jealousy, in its various forms, can strain even the strongest of bonds. Some forms of jealousy create not just emotional barriers, but also spiritual ones. These barriers are not built with bricks or open hostility, but through silences, pauses, and carefully chosen words.

Sometimes, you might feel an invisible weight that makes it hard to enjoy your happiness. You may start to doubt that you deserve your blessings. You might even wonder if your brightness is too much for others to handle. This spiritual struggle is very real, and it's important to see it clearly for what it is. Jesus Himself sat at tables where betrayal was brewing. He continued to speak truth, to break bread, and to love deeply even when He knew hearts around Him were hardened by envy.

His example teaches us that our response to such subtle resistance is not to retreat or to mute our testimony, but to remain grounded in our identity as God's beloved and in our commission to shine. When you feel that unspoken judgment, you can refuse to let it define you. You can speak the words of Psalm 139 over your life, reminding yourself that you are, *"fearfully and wonderfully made,"* cherished not for who you are, but for who you genuinely are. You can choose to meet reluctance with kindness and understanding.

If you're feeling a distance in your connections, the antidote is meaningful conversation. By 'meaningful conversation', we mean a dialogue that is open, honest, and non-confrontational. You might reach out with something like, *"I've noticed a shift since that compliment, and I truly miss the openness we shared. Can we talk about it?"* Embracing such vulnerability does not weaken your stance; rather, it cultivates deeper trust. It brings clarity to the lurking spirit of envy and, just like sunlight, drives away the shadows.

Language of the Soul — Emotions vs. Feelings

"The heart knows its own bitterness, and no one else can share its joy."
— Proverbs 14:10, NIV

Jealousy often starts with a physical sensation, like a racing heartbeat or a sinking feeling in the stomach. These emotions are instinctive reactions that trigger narratives in our minds. We then interpret these sensations, creating stories around them, such as *"They don't deserve that"* or *"Their success will harm me."* By recognising and understanding these emotions, we can better manage our reactions and mindsets, rather than letting them dictate our actions. When we miss this distinction, we may dismiss essential signals from our inner selves as mere moodiness or oversensitivity.

We might say, *"I'm experiencing insecurity today,"* and move on without pausing to ask, *"What message is this emotion trying to convey?"* Without this moment of reflection, jealousy can take hold, shaping our self-image and our relationships. It convinces us that we are either inadequate or threatened, leading us to act on these false beliefs, withdrawing in fear or competing for perceived worth. Jesus felt deep emotions. He cried for Jerusalem, showed compassion for hungry crowds, and suffered in the Garden of Gethsemane. However, He did not let His feelings control His actions. Instead, He shared His feelings with His Father, allowing God's perspective to change His distress into obedience and His sorrow into hope. We are also encouraged to bring our true emotions to God. In His presence, His truth can change how we feel, give us hope, and guide us in our lives.

Jealousy: Emotion, Feeling, or Force?

Beyond these obvious signs, jealousy can also act as a negative force, often influenced by spiritual factors, trying to create division, confusion, and doubt among people. Understanding the different types of jealousy is important for gaining awareness and insight. When jealousy arises as an emotion, it feels immediate and natural. Our heart races when a colleague receives praise, or a tight knot forms in our chest as those around us celebrate someone's achievement. These moments can catch us off guard but often pass quickly.

They serve as our soul's alarm bell, alerting us to deeper insecurities or unresolved wounds. As an emotion, jealousy constructs a story we tell ourselves: *"She was chosen today, so I'll be forgotten tomorrow,"* or *"If he is recognised for his talent, who will notice mine?"*

However, when jealousy functions as a force, it transcends personal sensitivity and mental narratives, invading communal and spiritual realms. It can seem like a weight pressing down on a group's unity, transforming constructive feedback into damaging criticism and turning encouragement into suspicion. Jealousy may manifest through whispered questions about motives or retreat into silence, leaving some voices unheard.

Scripture warns us that where envy thrives, confusion and every kind of evil follow. This means jealousy as a force not only disturbs individual hearts; it paves the way for deeper spiritual discord. It plants seeds of bitterness that grow into strife, dividing families, discouraging leaders, and dampening the spirit of genuine connections. Identifying jealousy in all its forms needs spiritual discernment. This is the ability to perceive and understand spiritual truths and realities. We begin by paying attention to our physical reactions and analysing the narratives we attach to them. We ask ourselves, *"Is this merely a human reaction, or is something deeper at play?"*

Then, we bring our feelings into the light of God's truth, commanding any spiritual influences that oppose His peace to leave. From emotion to feeling to force, the progression of jealousy reveals its true danger and the urgency of addressing it fully. The same Spirit that exposes darkness also brings healing and unity. By inviting Jesus into each aspect of our jealousy, our physical reactions, our mental narratives, and any spiritual strongholds, we allow His freedom to flourish, washing away every trace of envy with the abundance of His love. While all emotions arise in the body, some carry deeper spiritual weight, like jealousy. A passing thought of envy may seem harmless. Still, when we allow that thought to linger and evolve into suspicion or resentment, it becomes a spiritual stronghold that must be addressed with urgency.

Think of a garden. A single weed might seem small and harmless, but if you ignore it, its roots will spread and choke the valuable plants. In the same way, a small feeling of jealousy can grow if not addressed. It can take over our thoughts, words, and relationships, turning us from happy participants of God's story into anxious competitors. Scripture does not treat jealousy lightly. Proverbs 14:30 compares envy to rot in the bones, emphasising that unchecked jealousy deteriorates our spiritual health. When we dismiss jealousy as *"just a feeling,"* we enable it to grow into bitterness, strife, and actions we may later regret.

PART TWO: ROOTS OF JEALOUSY

Group Dynamics

When one team member achieves success, it can create a ripple effect, impacting the dynamics and morale of the entire team. Others might feel insecure or doubt their own contributions, leading them to withdraw or become less engaged. This can be due to unspoken questions like *"Why didn't my idea get attention?"* or *"Am I being left out?"* Rather than celebrating the success, team members might protect their self-worth by pulling back.

To improve this atmosphere, the team can try a different approach. After each success, everyone shares one thing they learned and one area they want to improve. This keeps everyone involved and helps see success as a shared journey, not as a threat. It shows that when one person shines, it helps everyone grow and makes each team member feel valued.

Family gatherings can become tense when one member achieves something notable, like graduating with honours or getting engaged. The mood shifts, conversations become more serious, and compliments are scarce. Although no one openly admits to envy, it can still be felt.

Subtle changes, like delayed congratulations or awkward pauses when mentioning the person's name, can create a strained atmosphere. Over time, this can become the norm, affecting who feels included or excluded.

To counter this in families, set aside time for everyone, no matter their age or situation, to share their recent achievements, big or small. These could be as simple as passing a test, learning to cook a new dish, or finishing a personal project. This helps make celebrations inclusive, ensuring everyone's milestones matter and no one's success dims another's light. When we choose to be honest and hold ourselves accountable instead of comparing, the dynamic shifts. Jealousy loses its power.

Cultural and Spiritual Frameworks That Feed Jealousy

Jealousy does not happen randomly. It grows from the cultural and spiritual environment we live in, shaped by the values and beliefs we learned earlier in life. We begin to understand which accomplishments get praise, which behaviours earn respect, and which successes define our social status. In many families and communities, visible achievements are seen as markers of success, like good grades, nice homes, or public recognition. When these outside measures become the norm, they create a ranking system.

Those at the top get constant approval, while others often feel like they are falling behind. For example, in a small community where success is based on home size or car brand, if a neighbour renovates their house or buys a new car, it sends a message about their social status. Other neighbours may feel a mix of admiration and inadequacy, comparing their own progress to that of their neighbour. In this way, seeing someone else's achievements can confirm our feelings of stagnation or failure.

In spiritual communities, visible accomplishments can become a measure of faith or closeness to God, leading to feelings of insecurity and jealousy. Instead of addressing their own inadequacies, people might question the value of others' achievements, masking their jealousy as spiritual wisdom. This can hinder personal growth and distort the true meaning of spiritual development. To address jealousy, we need to identify the cultural values and expectations we've accepted as true. We should examine the external achievements we've been taught to admire and the signals of belonging we've internalised. We also need to identify the spiritual beliefs we've accepted, such as thinking that God's favour is often assumed to be proven by visible success or by blessings that arrive on a predictable timeline.

This process of identification can be challenging but rewarding. It requires reflecting on our beliefs, seeking diverse viewpoints, and having open conversations with others. Once we identify these narratives, we can challenge them by questioning their truth, exploring other views, and promoting a broader understanding of success.

By bringing these hidden beliefs to light, we can start replacing them with truth. We can remind ourselves that God's ways aren't limited to human ideas of success. His support is not only for the most visible ministry, the largest home, or the most recognised achievements. Instead, He values unique gifts, callings, and different growth seasons. When one neighbour's garden blooms, it doesn't lessen the potential for another's roses to flourish; it reminds us that the same Gardener nurtures each yard uniquely.

Communities can work against jealousy by broadening their definitions of success. A neighbourhood association could celebrate not just the grandest renovations but also quiet acts of kindness, like a neighbour providing meals for a sick family. Similarly, a church could honour not only large services or charismatic speakers but also dedicated volunteers who pray with individuals one-on-one behind the scenes.

This shift in focus from public displays to genuine, often unseen acts of care and faithfulness empowers everyone in the community and offers hope for a more inclusive story of success.

When we redefine success in cultural and spiritual narratives this way, jealousy loses its grip. Rather than seeing success as limited and competitive, we begin to view life as a rich tapestry where each person's unique calling is woven together by God's hand. In this new perspective, celebrating another's progress becomes a source of gratitude, strengthens community ties, and enhances our joy. We can actively celebrate diverse achievements, making the community stronger and more supportive.

The Psychology of Jealousy — The Mind as the Battlefield

Jealousy often starts with a simple thought: *"She got the opportunity I wanted*" or *"He is showing his art while mine stays hidden."* At first, these things seem small, but our minds take them seriously. Think of your mind as a workshop filled with tools, some tools build your confidence, while others hurt your self-worth. When you notice someone else's success, that thought is like picking up a new tool. On its own, it is not good or bad; it just shows something you care about.

However, if you keep thinking, *"If only I had her confidence"* or *"Why does his work connect with people more than mine?"* that tool becomes harmful. Each repeated thought sharpens a jagged edge, creating deep grooves of self-doubt in your mind.

You might start to expect rejection; you picture moments where your ideas get ignored, conversations break down, or you don't receive praise.

These imagined failures can feel so real that they alter your behaviour, causing you to hesitate before trying new things and hold back your talents.
Often, these patterns come from childhood wounds. You might have learned that love and approval depended on how well you performed. Good marks (Grades), winning competitions, or good behaviour may have seemed important for affection. These lessons stick with you: *"Only perform well enough to be loved."* Even years later, you still carry that worn-out belief. So, when someone else succeeds, it feels like your *"affection account"* empties.

The good news is that you can reorganise this workshop. Each time you catch yourself in overthinking, you have a choice. You can keep the harmful tool, or you can set it aside for a better one: a line from Scripture, a reminder of your worth, or a memory of when you helped others without recognition.

For example, when you think, *"She was chosen over me,"* pause and say aloud, *"God's wisdom isn't about picking favourites; He gives each of us a unique purpose."* Saying these words helps you identify and use new tools when the old thoughts come back.

Over time, these affirmations can become habits. The deep grooves that led you to jealousy will fade, replaced by paths that encourage a secure identity and a celebration of others. Your mind can change from a battleground to a well-organized workshop where each tool has a purpose. Write down the thought, and respond with a written truth:

By repeating this exercise, you retrain your mind to see which tools lift you up, and which ones drag you down. When you feel the pull of envy, you will instinctively reach for your true response instead of slipping back into old criticism.

By changing your mindset this way, you will stop being driven by fear or the need for approval. You will realise that your worth does not depend on praise but on being known and loved by God. This shift brings true peace; your mind will no longer be a battleground of self-criticism but a workshop of renewed purpose, where your thoughts are guided by truth and placed in order. This is not just a transformation journey, but a path to a more peaceful and purposeful life.

The Spiritual Nature of Jealousy

The Bible addresses jealousy seriously. It states, *"Where envy and selfish ambition exist, there is disorder and every evil work."* This verse reveals that jealousy not only causes emotional discomfort but also suggests that unchecked envy fosters an environment conducive to chaos, mistrust, and destructive patterns in our lives and communities. When jealousy goes unexamined, it evolves from a momentary emotion into something that influences our choices, relationships, and spiritual well-being.

At its core, jealousy may cause doubts about God's character. We might not say it aloud, but when we see others being blessed while we suffer being unnoticed. We may start to perceive someone else's answered prayer or success as proof that God is withholding something from us. Over time, our attitude shifts from waiting in faith to harbouring resentment.

This shift can happen subtly. This emotion can be disguised under a veil of etiquette or mindfulness, beneath the surface, it often takes the form of jealousy, not just emotionally, but also spiritually. The problem extends beyond feelings of exclusion; it leads us to question how God distributes His grace and opportunities.

For instance, a member who consistently leads successful prayer groups might inadvertently cause jealousy among others who sense their own contributions are not as recognised.

Jealousy should be viewed as a spiritual issue rather than just a personality flaw or minor attitude problem. It reveals our beliefs about God's character. If we see His love as limited, we may end up competing for it. If we think His blessings are few, we might try to earn them. However, when we recognise God's nature as generous, abundant, and deeply personal, we can free ourselves from many burdens.

To address jealousy spiritually, the first step is to confess your feelings honestly. This goes beyond simply admitting your jealousy; it involves accepting what this emotion reveals about your faith. You might pray, *"God, I see that I have questioned your goodness. I have looked at others and assumed you have forgotten me. I have measured your love for me by your successes. Help me to trust you again."* This kind of confession does not bring shame; it paves the way for spiritual healing.

Once you have confessed, it is important to renew your mind-set. Intentionally replace thoughts of scarcity with truths from Scripture. When you feel there is not enough to go around, remember, *"My God will supply all your needs according to His riches in glory"* (Philippians 4:19).

When you think it is unfair that someone else received what you longed for, hold on to the truth that *"God delights to give good gifts to His children"* (Matthew 7:11). These are not just words; they are truths that reshape how we understand God's heart toward us, providing a solid foundation for our renewed mind-set.

Another effective way to respond to jealousy is to practice generosity. Instead of retreating or becoming passive-aggressive toward those we envy, we can choose to bless them. We can pray for their continued success, offer encouragement, or even support their efforts. This is not always easy, but it can be a transformative process. When we celebrate someone else in the area where we feel insecure, we break the grip jealousy has on our hearts. This act of kindness serves as a spiritual resistance, a conscious effort to resist the negative influence of jealousy, inviting God's peace into our lives.

To acknowledge jealousy as a spiritual issue does not mean we over spiritualise every emotional struggle. It reminds us how profoundly jealousy can distort our view of God and others. We should acknowledge that comparison is not a neutral behaviour; it indicates a deeper spiritual battle that affects our relationship with God, our self-esteem, and how we treat those around us.

In many faith traditions, including Christianity, jealousy is viewed as a destructive force that can harm both our relationships and spiritual growth. Scripture emphasizes the importance of guarding our hearts against jealousy, promoting instead virtues like contentment, gratitude, humility, and love. By cultivating these traits, we can better resist the temptation to compare ourselves to others and overcome jealousy. It is also crucial to recognise that jealousy has often been conveyed as a sense of connection. Many refer to it as a "spirit," not to exaggerate, but because it can feel like a presence that lingers, influencing our perceptions and shaping our actions.

Whether this idea is taken literally or metaphorically depends on one's beliefs. Nonetheless, the point remains: jealousy carries significant spiritual weight. It can change atmospheres, shape communities, and either bring us closer to God or push us away, depending on our response. Understanding jealousy as a spiritual concern encourages us to respond with honesty and hope. We do not need to deny or downplay it; we should acknowledge it openly. We must expose it, confess what it reveals, and allow God to transform our perspective. Jealousy does not exclude us from God's love; instead, it highlights how much we need it. When we bring even this emotion into His presence, we open ourselves to healing, restoration, and a deeper trust in the One whose blessings are abundant and perfectly timed

PART THREE: PERSONAL AND RELATIONAL WOUNDS

When Jealousy Lives Within

Sometimes, jealousy isn't about envying others, but a quiet, internal struggle. It can manifest as a heaviness or a subtle shift in mood, often triggered by social media or seeing others receive recognition. A seemingly innocent moment can spark self-doubt and a nagging question: "Why her?"

This internal jealousy often stems from deeply ingrained narratives that tell us we're not enough or behind. These thoughts become emotional scripts that shape our interactions and self-presentation. If left unchecked, they can lead to self-doubt, declining opportunities, or overcompensating to the point of perfectionism. This fear of not being lovable unless we're flawless can drive our actions and decisions.

It can emerge in everyday moments, like when we feel disregarded or unappreciated, and it can subtly shape our perceptions of love, identity, and our place in the world. Over time, it can even affect our understanding of God's love, leading us to wonder if we're included in His promises or if His love is conditional. This type of jealousy can become a persistent undertone in our minds, quietly influencing our thoughts and emotions.

Inherited Patterns

Jealousy often develops subtly over time, becoming a part of who we are without us even realizing it. It's not usually something we're directly taught, but rather something we pick up from the environment we grew up in the tone, emotional climate, and unspoken expectations. It's passed down through behaviours and attitudes, forming in the gaps of what wasn't said or the emotional support that was withheld. This can shape our understanding of love, acceptance, and self-worth in profound ways.

Many of us, regardless of our backgrounds, can relate to growing up in environments where love and attention were scarce. Praise might have come only when we succeeded, affection could have been tied to our performance or behaviour, and only certain types of achievements may have been celebrated. Even if our caregivers had good intentions, the underlying message often became that being good or successful was the path to being noticed and, by extension, loved.

This emotional atmosphere serves as the foundation for how we view ourselves and others. Even before we understood what envy meant, we were being trained to assess our worth based on how others responded to us. We learned whether love was

available to us unconditionally or whether we had to earn it by standing out.
For many, jealousy doesn't start in adulthood; it often manifests as competition at work or feelings of envy when watching friends succeed. It usually begins in early childhood, within the private emotional world of a child who feels invisible. It takes root in the quiet efforts that go unnoticed, in the child who is consistently responsible but rarely praised, in the one who does well but is never singled out, and in the one who sees others celebrated without restraint and silently asks, "Why not me?"

These early encounters shape our belief system, often unconsciously, around the idea that our worth is tied to visibility and recognition. We may believe we need to stand out, work harder, and constantly prove ourselves to be loved and valued. Over time, these thoughts solidify into deep-seated convictions, like needing to outshine others to matter.

When these patterns are established, jealousy can emerge, often masquerading as overthinking, second-guessing, or disinterest. Sometimes, it hides behind unspoken words, masking the true pain – a deep-seated belief that love and value are conditional and must be earned. This pain stems from childhood experiences where love and attention felt scarce and conditional. Over time, this could bring about an emotional state of survival. We begin doing things or developing ourselves not just to grow or serve, but to be seen.

We build emotional shield around our hearts, learning to compete subtly, work harder, be agreeable, or excel in our pursuits, not only out of passion but also to secure a sense of belonging that should have been unconditional from the start.

It's completely fine to “grieve” about what you didn't receive. If you didn’t get praise, if support was conditional, or if others didn’t notice your uniqueness, that's valid. You are no longer the child who had to earn love, the teenager hoping to be recognised, or the adult comparing yourself to others. You are not behind. You are not invisible.

Your path is not wrong. You are seen and loved for who you are, not just for what you do. Even before you achieved anything impressive or received labels like “gifted” or “good,” you were already seen and loved deeply. This focus on your worth should help you feel valued and important.

Healing is a journey, not a destination. You don’t need to rush or have perfect feelings. What matters is your honesty and your willingness to accept that your worth is secure. You belong, even when you are not the centre of attention, and your voice matters, even if others have not heard it yet.

Reciprocal Jealousy

Reciprocal jealousy often starts with subtle cues, like unspoken tension or slight changes in behaviour. Unlike one-sided jealousy, it develops between two people who both feel insecure or uncertain. When one person withdraws or becomes cautious, the other picks up on it and responds with similar emotions, creating a cycle where each person's reactions fuel the other's fears. This can lead to a dynamic of mutual suspicion and emotional distance.

This dynamic can arise in various contexts: workplaces, close friendships, ministry teams, and even families. Picture two individuals who once collaborated openly, thriving in a supportive relationship where they freely shared ideas. Then, something shifts. One person may gain recognition or visibility, not necessarily a promotion or public praise, but a subtle boost in trust, inclusion, or compliments. The other observes this change and, rather than celebrating, begins to hold back. This response does not stem from bitterness but from uncertainty: "What does this change mean for me? Am I still valued? Has my contribution been dismissed?"

This hesitation often goes unspoken but is still felt. The celebrated individual senses the change, detecting coldness or a more reserved tone and noticing conversations that no longer flow easily.

As a result, they, too, withdraw, not out of a desire to create distance, but from confusion regarding their standing.

They wrestle with concerns about how their success might have altered perceptions. Instead of joy, they now associate their accomplishments with potential loss in the relationship. In this unspoken exchange, jealousy assumes a relational dimension. It ceases to be simply one person struggling with insecurity; both individuals now adjust to a perceived imbalance, each silently asking questions that the other cannot hear: "Do you still care about me?" "Can I be happy for you without losing my place?" "Will we ever return to our previous dynamic?"

This mutual tension can be emotionally exhausting, requiring constant interpretation of each other's silences, responses, and behaviours. Every moment of distance, tonal shift, or delayed reply becomes a signal that something has changed.

A relationship that was once based on trust may now feel like a careful negotiation, where both individuals are compelled to shield themselves from emotional exposure. The emotional toll of this constant vigilance and interpretation is significant, often leading to feelings of exhaustion and emotional strain.

What complicates reciprocal jealousy is how it positions both individuals defensively. Even when neither started with bad intentions, the instinct for self-protection can make every reaction feel personal. One person's caution might be seen as criticism; the other's silence could be perceived as withdrawal. As no one directly addresses the discomfort, the relationship becomes emotionally constrained. This defensive positioning can unintentionally lead to misinterpretations and further strain the relationship.

Breaking this cycle requires someone to embrace vulnerability by openly discussing what lies beneath the surface. A conversation might begin with: "I've sensed a shift between us, and I'm unsure how to respond. I care about our relationship, and I don't want any unresolved feelings." When vulnerability leads the dialogue, it often reveals that both people face similar fears: the fear of being left behind, the fear of becoming irrelevant, or the fear that achievement will always come at a cost. Open dialogue, when approached with courage and empathy, can be a powerful tool in resolving reciprocal jealousy and strengthening the relationship.

Reciprocity is closely tied to the human need for security and a sense of belonging. When those needs feel threatened, even unintentionally, jealousy can disguise itself as caution or withdrawal.

However, beneath these behaviours lies an unspoken question: "Do I still matter to you as I once did?"

To heal this dynamic, honesty is necessary, not just about; the changes that have occurred but also about how those changes have affected both parties internally. Both individuals need to confront what they have felt without expressing it verbally. They should strive to see each other not as rivals or replacements but as individuals navigating their emotions.

It's vital to recognise that relationships evolve. Success, personal growth, recognition, and shifting roles are a natural part of life. Still, these changes need not lead to disconnection. When handled with humility and care, they can create opportunities for deeper understanding. Jealousy loses its hold not when we force ourselves to feel differently but when we acknowledge the reality, invite honest dialogue, and choose connection over silence.

Reciprocal jealousy doesn't have to ruin a relationship. Still, it will distort it unless someone is courageous enough to bridge the discomfort and say, "I still value you. Can we talk?"

Silent Competitions and the Weight of Being Seen

In many settings, like shared workspaces, team projects, or family gatherings, a subtle undercurrent of competition can emerge. When someone achieves something notable, it can trigger discomfort in others, often stemming from internal struggles with self-worth or feelings of being underestimated. This can lead to hesitation, guarded interactions, and emotional distance, causing people to tread carefully and play it safe. Over time, this dynamic can weaken the openness and camaraderie that once defined the space. This pattern of hidden tension is what we call the 'underlying current of distinction'.

As we progress, we will examine how the pressure to compare can show up in many areas of life, often in subtle ways. At work, it might look like ambition but undermine teamwork. With friends, it can lead to avoidance and doubts, damaging emotional safety. At home, it can cause tension between siblings or partners, showing up as frustration or withdrawal. In families, old patterns of competition can persist. Even in spiritual communities, roles and titles can spark insecurity. And on social media, constant exposure to others' successes can make people feel invisible.

Each chapter to come will go deeper into these unique spaces, to understand how jealousy functions in different relationships. The aim is to explore how healing, maturity, and honest reflection can disrupt its influence and restore peace. By the end of this journey, you will have a deeper understanding of these dynamics and how to navigate them in your own life.

The Social Media Comparison Trap

Scrolling through social media these days can quickly turn into a journey that leaves us feeling like outsiders. It is easy to be swept away by the constant stream of everyone else's perfectly curated moments, those shiny announcements, dreamy vacations, and stunning achievements that seem to come effortlessly. What we often forget is that these highlights don't show the whole story. Behind those polished images lie disappointments, tears, and the loneliness that often lingers even after the praise fades away.

As we soak in these highlight reels, it’s hard not to compare our everyday lives, which may feel messy and unfinished, to the seemingly perfect lives of others. We start measuring our worth and progress against their curated displays, and before long, a quiet jealousy forms.

The Reality Behind the Highlights

The truth is what we see on social media is just a slice of someone's life. Even the brightest, happiest photo can hide the deep doubts or struggles that lie beneath. That new venture may come with pressure and self-doubt. A glowing testimony might be shadowed by unspoken pain or hidden challenges. Yet none of that makes it to the feed.

When we only focus on the visible, we risk undervaluing the unseen work God is doing in our own lives. We forget that real growth often happens in the quiet, away from the spotlight. Social media tempts us to stack our less-than-perfect reality against someone else's edited highlight reel. If our journey feels slow or unnoticed, it's easy to feel left behind. Jealousy has a sneaky way of creeping in, too. It doesn't wait for social gatherings or conversations; it can strike the moment we pick up our phones. An engagement announcement, a new car, or even a graduation picture. You might double-tap in genuine support while feeling a small pang inside that asks, "Why not me?"

That feeling isn't malicious; it's just the ache of comparing our lives to those we admire. We start to wonder why our breakthroughs seem so far away, why our progress feels unremarkable. While social media didn't create jealousy, it certainly nurtures it by making it easy to compare our messy reality to someone else's best moments.

We miss the backstory, the therapy session that followed that glowing photo, the silent struggles behind a joyful vacation, or the hidden burdens beneath those inspiring captions. Instead, we tend to measure ourselves against these edited snippets, equating visibility with worth. When our journey isn't seen, we start to doubt its value.

Such differences can lead to questions that weigh heavily on our faith: "God, have you forgotten me?" ""Why is she marrying now when I'm still waiting?" If left unchecked, these doubts can grow into envy, self-pity, and exhaustion, and we might even start to question God's goodness. All the while, a hidden battle rages within us, stealing joy and confidence. But there's another way to approach this.

Before you dive into your scrolling, take a moment to pause and invite God into that space. Say a quiet prayer: "Lord, I'm grateful for the good things in her life, and I trust you're working in mine too." Don't let your worth be dictated by likes or followers; remember that everyone's social media presence is just a highlight reel, not the full story. Your value is defined in God's eyes, not by the metrics of social media. He sees every late-night prayer, every moment of obedience, and every tear shed in silence, and He is always close.

So, release the urge to perform. You don't need to prove anything. Let go of the pressure to look perfect, understanding that God's love for you isn't contingent on your image. Break free from the cycle of scrolling, comparing, feeling inadequate, doubting God, retreating, and then scrolling again. Celebrate others' victories, bless them in their joy, and remember that God's blessings are abundant. This way, you can embrace your own unique journey, moving forward with peace and purpose, secure in the knowledge that God's timing for you is perfect.

Jealousy in the Workplace

Workplace jealousy can thrive in environments where success feels like a zero-sum game, conveying the unspoken message that only one person can win at a time. This type of jealousy can be hard to spot, but it can change the workplace atmosphere. Colleagues might start withholding information or become hesitant to give feedback. What was once a collaborative environment can become tense and strained, with underlying resentment affecting team dynamics. As these tensions grow, their effects ripple through the office. Casual coffee-break chats become stilted, with colleagues opting for safe topics rather than risking exposure to envy or disappointment. Morale takes a hit: those who feel forgotten may disengage quietly, performing just enough to meet expectations. In contrast, some begin updating their resumes instead of enduring another day of unrecognised effort.

Underlying this tension are several familiar dynamics. Sometimes, resentment evolve from proximity, when the person you are comparing yourself to shares a similar role or knowledge. When someone with a comparable background receives praise or recognition, it is likely to feel more personal and trigger self-doubt, even if you respect them. Leadership may unintentionally fuel competition. When managers use jealousy to boost productivity, asking questions such as, “Why can’t you perform as well as them?”, or rely on one individual for visibility while neglecting the rest, they could damage morale and undermine the team’s effectiveness. Such actions foster an environment where resentment is likely to thrive, leading employees to believe that attention must be earned at the cost of their colleagues.

The workplace shifts from focusing on shared goals to nurturing unspoken rivalries. The consequences of workplace jealousy are rarely limited to the individual experiencing it; they often extend to those around them. Jealousy spreads and erodes team cohesion. People withdraw, hesitate to contribute, or start questioning each other’s intentions. In some cases, it escalates into gossip, passive-aggressive behaviour, or outright resentment. More commonly, the damage is subtle. The effects of workplace jealousy are not limited to the envied. They can be felt by the envious as well.

They may sense a chill in their relationships, feel excluded from conversations, or even downplay their own achievements to avoid discomfort. When success becomes a source of unease, it loses its shine. Jealousy places a heavy burden on those who feel trapped, those who complete their tasks and show up consistently, and wonder if their moment will ever arrive. With time, this feeling can lead to emotional fatigue. It’s possible that they might stop striving, not from laziness, but because relentless effort without recognition is exhausting. The workplace becomes a space of silent losses, not only job roles, but also connections, value, and self-esteem.

These impacts affect more than only individuals. When jealousy infiltrates team culture, the entire organisation suffers. Productivity declines, innovation stalls, and ideas are kept close rather than shared. Colleagues become more invested in protecting their positions than in collaborative efforts. Good employees, whether envied or envious, begin seeking exits. However, the presence of jealousy does not signify a broken team or an irreparable culture. It serves as a call for reflection at all levels. Jealousy is not just an emotion to be avoided; it's a signal. It points to uncertainty about worth, confusion about decision-making, or fear of being ignored.
While it doesn’t have to be excused, it certainly demands acknowledgment. Only by acknowledging it can we take meaningful steps to address the underlying issues.

Jealousy among Friends

Friendship is meant to be a space where mutual support, joy, and trust are cultivated. It is a place where people celebrate each other's milestones, speak honestly about their challenges, and walk together through seasons of growth. What often begins as quiet admiration for a friend's talents or opportunities can gradually turn into questions about one's own worth considering that friend's success.

A person may publicly celebrate a friend's achievements while privately wrestling with thoughts such as, "Why isn't this happening for me?" or "What does their progress say about my stagnation?" This emotional shift is not always malicious or intentional; in many cases, it comes from deeply rooted insecurities, unmet desires, or patterns of comparison that have never been examined.

When one person progresses and the other feels left behind, the dynamic of the friendship subtly shifts.
Biblical history provides us with valuable lessons on this emotional reality. One of the earliest examples of jealousy in a close relationship is found in the story of Cain and Abel. Genesis 4:4-5 tells us, "*The Lord looked with favour on Abel and his offering, but on Cain and his offering He did not look with favour. So, Cain was furious, and his face was downcast.*" Abel's offering was accepted, while Cain's was not.

Instead of speaking to God about his hurt or seeking guidance on how to grow, Cain allowed his jealousy to grow. This jealousy ultimately ended in violence, but God's warning was clear before it escalated: "*Sin is crouching at your door; it desires to have you, but you must rule over it*" (Genesis 4:7). The issue began not with outward aggression, but with inward comparison and emotional displacement. This story, and many others in the Bible, serve as a guide for us to recognise and address jealousy in our own lives. In friendships today, the consequences of jealousy can be emotionally devastating. It can shift the tone of a relationship.

A friend who once offered support may now respond with delayed replies, subtle withdrawal, or disengaged enthusiasm. Communication becomes guarded. Accomplishments are shared with disclaimers or not shared at all for fear of causing tension. It becomes easier to share burdens than to share joy, leading to emotional distance, not due to a lack of love, but because celebrating each other has become complicated. This destructive nature of jealousy underscores the urgency to address it in our friendships.

Jealousy may appear as when one friend suddenly highlights their own accomplishments in response to another's good news, not to celebrate together, but to rebalance the emotional scale. Another might start downplaying the importance of the other's success.

Although these actions may not be fully conscious, they reveal a heart that feels threatened rather than safe in the friendship. This dynamic is not new. Consider King Saul's relationship with David. When David killed Goliath and the people celebrated him, the women sang, "*Saul has slain his thousands, and David his tens of thousands*" (1 Samuel 18:7). From that moment, Saul's attitude toward David changed. Verse 9 states, "And from that time on, Saul kept a close eye on David." What began as trust, when Saul welcomed David into his service, was now tainted by suspicion and competition. Although David remained loyal, Saul could no longer rejoice in David's victories; he feared being replaced, which is often the underlying root of jealousy in close relationships. When one friend grows, the other may fear that such growth signifies separation or that their own value is diminished in comparison.

The spiritual aspect of jealousy becomes evident in this context. In 1 Corinthians 13:4, we are told that "*love does not envy.*" In its purest form, love can celebrate without hesitation. However, when insecurity takes root, love becomes conditional. Jealousy prompts individuals to question whether another's success threatens their own place in the relationship. This is not just an emotional reaction; it is a spiritual distortion of truth. Scripture teaches that God has a purpose and plan for each person (Jeremiah 29:11) and that He does not run out of favour or opportunity.

Yet jealousy whispers otherwise, introducing the fear that if someone else is advancing, there may be nothing left for you. This fear grows in environments where jealousy is normalised. In early friendships, especially those formed in youth or during shared life stages, there is often an unconscious expectation that both people will grow at the same pace. When that doesn't happen, the disparity in progress can be taken personally.

One may start to view the other's life as a mirror reflecting unfulfilled desires. However, envy distorts this reflection; it focuses on what someone else has and blinds one to their journey, even if it is unfolding more slowly or differently. Awareness of and opposition to this destructive habit is crucial in preventing jealousy from taking root in our friendships.

Scripture offers another example through the older brother in the parable of the prodigal son. When the younger brother returned and the father celebrated his return with a feast, the older brother grew angry. He said, "*All these years I've been slaving for you and never disobeyed your orders. Yet you never gave me even a young goat so I could celebrate with my friends*" (Luke 15:29). This response highlights the bitterness that can arise when jealousy takes hold and overshadows celebrations meant to unite.

The father replied gently, "*My son, you are always with me, and everything I have is yours*" (Luke 15:31). This passage addresses the emotional root of jealousy in friendships: the fear of being disregarded and the desire to be celebrated. God reassures us that His blessings for one person do not diminish what He has for another.

When jealousy goes unacknowledged in friendships, it alters the way people interact. One friend might become emotionally distant, while the other may start to feel guarded. Shared occurrences can begin to feel like a performance instead of genuine connections. What should be a joyful friendship may turn into a source of tension, transforming mutual growth into a quiet competition for validation.

Jealousy become visible from our insecurities. It raises questions such as: Am I enough? Am I being forgotten? Do I matter if I'm not achieving my goals? When these questions remain unanswered, a friend's happiness can unintentionally feel threatening. Though jealousy in friendship doesn't always destroy relationships, unaddressed feelings can alter them. It introduces fear where trust should exist, replaces support with competition, and hinders both friends from fully appreciating each other's presence and progress. Scripture encourages us to resist this pull, to love without jealousy, to rejoice with those who rejoice (Romans 12:15), and to trust that each person's journey unfolds in its rhythm under the guidance of a faithful God.

Jealousy in the Family

Even in loving families, jealousy often starts in small, everyday experiences. One child may excel academically and receive praise for their achievements, while a sibling who is kind, creative, or athletic might feel discounted and question why their strengths go unnoticed. A parent might proudly highlight one child's accomplishments to others but seldom acknowledges the efforts of the others.

Over time, these subtle patterns create emotional layers, some spoken and others silently felt. Jealousy in families can manifest as withdrawal or a sarcastic comment. At times, it creates a persistent sense that someone else is more loved, more celebrated, or more favoured. This feeling can occur between siblings and between parents and children, often influenced by how the family unknowingly distributes attention, praise, or expectations.

The biblical story of Cain and Abel serves as a powerful reminder that sibling jealousy is a universal thing. It illustrates how jealousy can first emerge in sibling relationships, with their rivalry catalysing devastating actions. This pattern has repeated itself throughout history, appearing in both stories and real life, where one child may feel overshadowed or constantly compared to their sibling.

Sibling jealousy can spring up as early as the birth of a younger sibling. An older child, once receiving their parents' undivided attention, might suddenly feel pushed aside. This change can lead to feelings of anger, clinginess, or emotional withdrawal. Some children might act out, not out of dislike for the new baby, but due to mourning the loss of being the sole focus of attention.

When children are close in age, reviews can become even more intense. They reach milestones at similar times, compete for attention in alike ways, and are expected to share space, toys, and aspects of their identities. If one consistently receives more praise, the other may internalise a belief that they are not good enough. Birth order significantly shapes these dynamics; firstborns might feel pressured to lead, middle children can feel invisible, and youngest children may receive more leniency. Regardless of birth order, the key to sibling jealousy lies in how each child feels about being recognised.

When a parent consistently praises one child's academic success while discounting another's creativity or emotional intelligence, it can sow the seeds of envy. The underestimate child may not express their feelings openly, but those emotions can fester. Over time, this emotional gap can widen into resentment.

At times, siblings who love one another deeply also know how to hurt each other the most. They are often closest in proximity and need, craving the same love and acknowledgement. This is why sibling jealousy can feel so personal and intense; it's not merely about toys or praise but about each child's place in the family's heart. During adolescence, these dynamics can become even more complicated. A sibling who enjoys more freedom, has more friends, or achieves more visible successes can trigger feelings of insecurity in the other.

Preventing jealousy from becoming permanent relies on how the home environment nurtures identity and recognition. If each child is affirmed for who they are, rather than solely for their achievements, the desire to compete may lessen. Celebrating differences instead of measuring them allows for individual growth. Parents play a crucial role here, not by treating children the same but by treating them fairly and recognising each child's uniqueness as equally valuable. This approach can pave the way for healing and growth, transforming jealousy into a catalyst for stronger family bonds. The story of Joseph in the Bible illustrates how favouritism can escalate sibling rivalry. Joseph was openly favoured by his father, which stirred envy among his brothers and led to betrayal. While most families may not reach such extremes, the core issue remains that when love feels uneven, relationships suffer.

Jealousy can flow not only between siblings but also between parents and children. Most parents deeply love their children and want the best for them. Yet, parents are also individuals with their histories, longings, and wounds. When a child achieves success, joy, or support that a parent never felt, it can evoke painful emotions. The parent might feel left behind or diminished by the child's accomplishments. It's important to acknowledge the complexity of these feelings, as doing so can validate the expertise of both parents and children.

A parent may observe their child thriving socially, academically, or professionally, experiencing a complex mix of pride and grief. This response isn't due to a lack of happiness for the child but rather because something in the parent's own story may feel unfulfilled. If these feelings go unacknowledged, they can manifest as criticism, emotional distance, or a tendency to undermine the child's joy. A parent might downplay achievements, pass special moments, or make seemingly small comments that carry significant weight, such as, "Must be nice to have everything handed to you," or "When I was your age, we didn't have that kind of support." These moments often surface from the past, rather than malice. A parent who never felt validated may struggle to develop a strong sense of self. Likewise, a parent who sacrificed their dreams might quietly resent seeing their child pursue their aspirations.

This does not mean they don't love their child; rather, their unmet needs resurface when they reflect on their child's life.

This complex dynamic can be challenging to address because parents are not typically expected to feel jealousy toward their children. Yet ignoring it only allows the feeling to fester. When a parent feels inadequate or left behind, the emotional environment of the home can be significantly affected. Children may begin to sense that their achievements make their parents uneasy. To avoid conflict, they might downplay their successes or hide their joy to safeguard a parent's feelings.

This dynamic can also shape how parents interact with each child. One may be favoured while the other becomes the target of the parent's frustrations or regrets. In some cases, one child may become the parent's "project," while other feels neglected. This creates confusion and ultimately division within the family.

From a Christian perspective, this kind of jealousy distorts the essence of parenthood. Parents are privileged to raise children who can reach higher, live fuller lives, and achieve greater freedom than they did. This isn't a failure; it's a legacy. When a child thrives, it should be seen as a continuation of God's goodness rather than a threat to the parent's values.

Scripture reminds us that "*children are a heritage from the Lord*" (Psalm 127:3), not a source of competition. As Paul writes, *love "does not envy, it does not boast, it is not proud*" (1 Corinthians 13:4). This applies to all family members, not just siblings. A parent grappling with jealousy is not a bad parent; they are human and may need to reflect on their unfulfilled desires.

Healing often begins when a parent chooses to invest in their personal growth. Starting a new hobby, setting new goals, or forming new friendships can alleviate feelings of loss or regret. Through prayer, self-reflection, and grace, a parent can learn to support their child without feeling diminished. Although it is challenging, it is achievable.

Jealousy in the home doesn't indicate a lack of love. Often, it means love has become intertwined with fear and unmet needs. However, this can be sorted out, not through perfect parenting or emotionless children, but through honesty, humility, and intentional love.

When families learn to affirm each member's worth, celebrate achievements without negative thoughts, and address their more complex emotions, jealousy loses its hold. A home becomes a space where everyone can shine without competition, grow without resentment, and love without fear of being replaced.

The goal isn't to eliminate envy; it's to cultivate strong relationships that can openly acknowledge and overcome these feelings.

Ultimately, jealousy within families is about more than possessions; it reflects who feels loved, recognised, and secure enough to be themselves. When families identify and address these emotional currents, they not only break destructive cycles but also foster an environment where everyone's growth is embraced, and no one must diminish their light to belong.

Jealousy in Marriage

Jealousy in marriage is an emotionally charged and spiritually disruptive process for couples. Within the sacred covenant of marriage, meant to embody trust, intimacy, and mutual commitment, jealousy can gradually undermine the foundation of the relationship. Unlike casual partnerships, marriage carries significant weight, encompassing emotional, physical, and spiritual connections, a reflection of God's relationship with His people. When jealousy enters this sacred space, it often manifests subtly, through suspicion, unspoken words, or emotional withdrawal. However, its effects can be profound, shaking trust, distorting love, and replacing unity with division.

In a marriage, jealousy may arise as a husband who silently resents his wife's professional achievements or a wife who withdraws emotionally when her husband seems more engaged with friends or ministry than with her. The root of jealousy often lies not in the other person's actions but in individual feelings. It typically arises as a response to perceived threats, fears of inadequacy, emotional neglect, or unresolved insecurities, echoing the sentiment: "If you thrive, where does that leave me?"

From a psychological standpoint, jealousy in marriage connects to issues of attachment, low self-esteem, or fear of abandonment. A spouse who has faced rejection or trauma in childhood or past relationships may subconsciously fear being replaced or unremarked. When their partner connects with others or excels in certain areas, these fears can resurface. If unaddressed, they can lead to controlling behaviours, accusations, or emotional manipulation, not out of spite, but as a means to protect against perceived loss.

Not all jealousy is harmful, however. There is a form of protective concern, sometimes referred to as righteous jealousy that aims to safeguard the integrity of the marriage. This type does not isolate or accuse; it asserts, "I care about our bond too much to let it be dismissed."

In Scripture, God describes Himself as a "jealous God" (Exodus 34:14), motivated not by insecurity but by the desire for exclusive covenant love. Likewise, marriage demands exclusivity, emotional safety, and boundaries that uphold the sacred connection.

The danger arises when protective care shifts into possessiveness. When one spouse begins to control the other's time, isolate them from friendships, or constantly question their integrity, jealousy transforms from a healthy aspect of the covenant into a corrosive presence. Trust turns to fear, and intimacy becomes a form of surveillance. This is where spiritual disruption takes hold. Instead of uniting in love and mutual freedom, the relationship is strained by suspicion and tension. The covenant evolves into a battleground for emotional survival.

Spiritually, jealousy in marriage illustrates a deeper misalignment. Covenant unity relies on mutual submission, humility, and love that prioritises the other's well-being. When jealousy governs a spouse's feelings, they stop seeing their partner through a lens of grace and begin to perceive them as a threat. This shift erodes the safety of the marriage; silence replaces vulnerability, and distance supplants affection. God's original design for marriage, where two become one flesh, is obscured by personal fears and unspoken competition.

Biblically, marital unity goes beyond cohabitation or shared responsibilities; it represents a spiritual joining. As Jesus stated, *"What God has joined together, let no one separate"* (Mark 10:9). Jealousy, if unregulated, serves as a dividing force. It distances hearts, disrupts peace, and can disconnect individuals from their sense of identity within the relationship. Over time, it fosters emotional isolation despite physical proximity.

Yet, covenant unity can be restored. Healing begins when one spouse asks, "What part of me feels unsafe or unseen?" The other must be willing to listen without defensiveness. Jealousy loses its hold when love is re-centred on God's truth: we are not in competition with one another but companions on a shared journey. Transparency and emotional repair, guided by God's truth, become essential tools to strengthen trust and rebuild a sense of safety. With these tools, every couple can find their way back to a healthy, jealousy-free marriage.

True covenant love allows each spouse the space to grow, succeed, and thrive without undermining the other's progress, achievements, or well-being. When jealousy surfaces, it signifies a need for deeper healing rather than pointing fingers. It invites couples to remember that covenant unity is not just about remaining together; it's about journeying together with their hearts aligned toward each other and God.

Emotional and Psychological Roots of Jealousy in Marriage

Jealousy in marriage rarely starts in the present. More often, it echoes unresolved wounds from the past. These emotional patterns can precede marriage by many years and become triggered when the intimacy of a covenant relationship brings old insecurities to the surface. One spouse may have grown up in an environment where affection was conditional or inconsistent, requiring them to earn love and attention. Another might carry the scars of betrayal from a previous relationship. Although they may seem to have moved on, their inner voice continues to urge them to protect against being replaced.

Within marriage, these emotional stories do not vanish; they intensify. The closeness of the relationship acts as a mirror, reflecting not only the spouse but also one's fears, needs, and unresolved pain. When one partner appears more confident, socially active, or spiritually grounded, the other might feel invisible or inadequate. Instead of acknowledging that feeling, it often manifests as suspicion or silent resentment. Jealousy typically expresses not "I'm afraid I'm not enough," but rather "Why you are focusing your attention elsewhere?" The visible reaction targets the spouse's behaviour, while the actual issue lies in the person's self-worth. Psychologically, jealousy is also tied to the feeling of inadequacy.

In marriage, assessments are not only made between spouses and outsiders; they frequently occur between the spouses themselves. One partner may feel they are contributing more or sacrificing more, silently resenting the other's rest, success, or happiness. Alternatively, one spouse might perceive themselves as falling behind and, rather than discussing that fear, allow it to simmer as a source of competition. As a result, the focus shifts from mutual growth to a quiet contest about who is more loved, admired, or valued.

These dynamics are not always apparent to outsiders. Some couples may seem connected and functioning well, yet internally, jealousy creates emotional distance. One partner might choose to withhold good news to avoid upsetting the other. Another could withdraw from being vulnerable, sensing that their spouse does not genuinely celebrate their achievements. Over time, joy becomes guarded, and emotional safety starts to diminish. The home, which should be a sanctuary, might feel like a space filled with quiet tension.

In some marriages, jealousy takes the form of control. A spouse might monitor the other's friendships, question how time is spent, or withdraw emotionally as a form of punishment. This behaviour often stems not from a desire to dominate but from an internal fear, fear of being left behind, not being chosen or losing significance in someone else's life. When fear drives a relationship, trust weakens. And as trust deteriorates, intimacy suffers. What makes jealousy especially harmful in marriage is that it often remains unspoken. Unlike anger or frustration, which typically surface during arguments, jealousy frequently hides beneath the surface. It may show itself through sarcasm, subtle criticisms, or emotional coldness. Because it is rarely addressed directly, it continues to fester. Years can pass with unresolved jealousy quietly eroding emotional connection until a moment of conflict reveals just how deep the hurt has become.

Spiritual Disruption: Jealousy's Impact on Covenant Unity

Marriage is not just a relationship; it is a spiritual covenant. When jealousy enters a marriage, it disrupts not only emotions and communication but also the spiritual atmosphere between two individuals joined before God. Jealousy is far from neutral; it carries confusion and suspicion, along with a subtle resistance to truth. When these dynamics linger, they begin to distort the essence of what marriage is meant to represent: trust, love, mutual respect, and spiritual harmony. Covenant requires more than just surface-level agreement on household matters; it demands a deep, heart-level understanding of who we are, what we carry, and how we are called to walk together. When jealousy enters the picture, maintaining this unity becomes increasingly complex.

One spouse may start to question the other's motives, while the other might feel compelled to hide parts of their life to avoid conflict. What once was a spiritual partnership, praying together, dreaming together, and interceding for one another, can turn into a quiet distance. Jealousy disrupts intercession, silences celebrations, and clouds spiritual clarity in recognising one's spouse. The person who was once viewed as a blessing may suddenly appear as a threat.

This change in perception is one of the most dangerous effects of jealousy: it alters how a person is regarded. Rather than seeing a spouse as a collaborator with a shared purpose, the jealous heart may perceive them as competition or even as untrustworthy. Spiritually, when vision becomes distorted, agreement is fractured. What used to flow freely between two hearts now feels obstructed. Communication can become strained, and unity may wither. This breakdown is not always explosive but is often deeply felt.

Jealousy can also create spiritual misalignment when one spouse begins to doubt their own identity and sense of purpose in light of the other's strengths. In a healthy marriage, one partner's strengths should uplift the other rather than instil fear. However, when jealousy takes root, these strengths can be misinterpreted as superiority. A wife's discernment might be dismissed as control, while a husband's leadership could be seen as arrogance.

A spouse's spiritual insight may be belittled or ignored, not because it is incorrect, but because it challenges an insecurity in the other. Where insecurity prevails, pride and rejection often follow. The jealous partner may dismiss spiritual conversations, resist encouragement, or disregard guidance, not out of disagreement with God, but from a struggle to accept support from someone they feel compelled to outshine.

This disconnection can also lead to accusations. Jealousy frequently accompanies fear, suspicion, and distorted thoughts. The mind may entertain ideas like, "Maybe they admire someone else more," or "They are growing spiritually without me." Instead of dismissing these thoughts, the jealous heart may allow them to take root. Over time, these thoughts can create strongholds, leading the spouse to be viewed through a lens of accusation rather than truth. The enemy thrives in environments of insecurity, sowing further division and making the imagined feel real, even when it is not.

From a spiritual warfare perspective, jealousy in marriage must be recognised for what it truly is: a doorway to confusion, emotional division, and broken unity. Scripture warns us that “envy and selfish ambition breed disorder and every evil practice”. This issue goes beyond external behaviours; it delves into the internal condition of the heart. When jealousy is allowed to exist, disorder inevitably follows.

The couple may begin to struggle with praying together and may feel spiritually dry and emotionally disconnected, uncertain about why peace seems to have eluded them. In reality, the spiritual bond of agreement has weakened.

Healing and Rebuilding: Restoring Unity Where Jealousy Has Taken Root

Healing from jealousy in marriage begins with honesty, with oneself and with God. It is not enough to avoid confrontation or downplay the emotion. Jealousy loses its power when it is named, exposed, and brought into the light. A spouse grappling with jealousy should not feel ashamed, but they must be willing to acknowledge what they are feeling. Without this vulnerability, the emotion remains hidden and festers. However, when brought forward with humility, healing can begin.

The goal is not to eradicate all insecurity permanently; every human endures moments of inadequacy, fear, or doubt. In marriage, the covenant provides a safe space for these fears to be acknowledged, discussed, and healed together. When one spouse openly states, "I've felt small next to your strength," or "I've struggled to celebrate your success because something within me feels left behind," it invites understanding and paves the way for spiritual restoration.

The person who hears a confession faces a choice: respond defensively or with compassion. Defensiveness builds walls, while compassion creates bridges. A spouse saying, "I see that in you, and your struggle does not threaten me," becomes a channel for God's healing. Marriage isn't meant to be a competition over who is more anointed, more successful, or more admired. It is a space for both partners to grow into their true selves, supported by each other.

Healing often involves spiritual repentance, not just for jealousy, but for the lies we believe to be true. Lies such as "I'm not enough," "I'll always be dismissed," and "There isn't room for both of us to shine." When these lies are internalised, they become agreements that must be broken. Through prayer and scripture, couples can dismantle these false beliefs and embrace God's vision for unity.

The Bible clearly states: *"Two are better than one…for if either of them falls, the one will lift his companion"* (Ecclesiastes 4:9-10). In a covenant relationship, one person's strength should uplift the other, not threaten them. When one thrives, neither is diminished; both become stronger. This truth is realised in a marriage when spouses choose to honour each other's gifts and callings without second thoughts.

Jealousy can fade with consistent affirmation. Couples must learn to speak into each other's identities, especially during tense moments. Phrases like "I'm not going anywhere," "I admire what God is doing in you," or "I want to grow with you, not apart from you" hold significant weight. They dispel shame, confront fear, and restore safety where confusion once existed.

Rebuilding unity also requires mindfulness of triggers. Many expressions of jealousy arise from minor issues rather than major betrayals. They often stem from repeated moments where one partner feels ignored. Taking the time to notice, affirm, and include one another in personal growth can help alleviate these feelings. Sharing spiritual insights, inviting each other into individual goals, and checking in emotionally are not only good practices but also vital safeguards for creating a positive atmosphere at home.

Couples may also need to pray together intentionally about the spirit behind jealousy. While some instances of envy may be emotional or psychological, others can have a spiritual basis. Jealousy can lead to confusion, resentment, and distance if left unaddressed. Together, couples can break the hold of jealousy by affirming, "We reject the spirit of competition, suspicion, and fear. We choose unity, truth, and honour." This approach does not require theatrical displays; it demands humility and a willingness to agree.

Ultimately, jealousy loses its grip when couples commit to building a culture of mutual celebration. This means recognising each other's successes, praying for breakthroughs, and preserving each other's dignity, even in moments of insecurity. It also involves the choice to believe in one another, even when fear whispers otherwise. Remember, a covenant is not something earned; it is a gift protected by love.

Cousin and Extended Family Jealousy

Extended family gatherings are often charged environments. Beneath the greetings, laughter, and ceremonial meals lies an unspoken layer of reviews. Aunts, uncles, and grandparents may not voice their thoughts, but they take note of them. Whose child has achieved more success? Who has married well? Which children are thriving, and which are struggling? These casual observations can breed jealousy, lingering long after the gathering has ended.

Over time, families adopt labels that shape how individuals are viewed. One cousin becomes "the responsible one," another "the free spirit," and yet another "the quiet achiever." Initially, these titles may seem harmless and even endearing. However, they begin to set expectations and create roles that are hard to escape. Such repetitive labelling assigns identities that were never freely chosen, subtly pitting family members against each other.

Jealousy in these contexts often does not manifest as open conflict. Instead, it manifests in subtle exclusions, such as a parent's offhand remark about a cousin's job being "real work" or a grandparent's excessive praise for one child while neglecting another. It is the way someone's success raises the bar for everyone else, not through inspiration, but through pressure.

In families with strong generational expectations, children are compared not only to their cousins but also to a standard usually rooted in the achievements of previous generations. Families unwittingly create environments where love and attention appear conditional, based on performance, conformity, or public image.

The emotional toll of these dynamics is significant. Even without spoken words, children absorb these structures. A cousin who receives constant praise learns that achievement is the path to belonging. Conversely, another cousin, whose talents differ or whose pace is slower, may start to feel forgotten. Some may strive harder, while others may withdraw, yet both carry emotional scars that can be deep and long-lasting.

Psychological and Sociological Roots of Cousin Rivalry

Psychologically, cousin rivalry closely resembles sibling rivalry in several ways. Although cousins may not live together, they often share emotional connections and have mutual observers, including parents, grandparents, and extended family members who frequently serve as judges and sometimes unintentionally provoke evaluations. This complex web of relationships and influences can intensify the feelings of rivalry.

Social juxtapositions theory suggests we assess our self-worth by measuring ourselves against those closest to us. Cousins, especially those of similar ages or backgrounds, often serve as key benchmarks. These analogies intensify when family members regularly celebrate one cousin's achievements while ignoring another's. Over time, a subtle hierarchy emerges: one cousin is the "golden child," another the "struggler," and yet another the "late bloomer." Once these roles are established, they become hard to change and significantly impact how children view themselves, both within the family and in the world at large. Sociologically, families are one of the first systems to shape identity. When a family assigns you a label, especially in relation to someone else, that identity does not remain confined to childhood; it influences how you perceive your value, success, and sense of belonging.

The cousin labelled as "brilliant" often feels pressured to uphold that title, sometimes sacrificing their well-being or authenticity. Meanwhile, the cousin who lacks recognition may cope by distancing themselves or overcompensating in other areas of life. These patterns intensify in families with intertwined boundaries, where each child's accomplishments reflect directly on the family's reputation. In such situations, one cousin's success can become another parent's measure of effective parenting. Without openly acknowledging it, these dynamics create a competition where love feels like a prize to be earned rather than an unconditional gift.

Effects on Identity Formation and Self-Worth

When a child is repeatedly compared to a cousin, they start to reshape their identity in response to those analogies. Regardless of whether the differences are verbal or implied, the underlying message is clear: "Who you are is not enough."

Some people attempt to reshape their identities entirely. They might choose new careers, aesthetics, or life paths, not out of true passion, but to dodge judgements. Others prefer to fade into the background, avoiding the risk of being judged and deemed inadequate. Whether a child becomes overly driven or emotionally detached, the core issue remains unchanged: they are not forming their identities based on truth.

Instead, they craft their sense of self in reaction to jealousy and conditional approval.

Even the favoured cousin faces challenges. Receiving praise for accomplishments can lead to a fragile sense of worth that collapses when they endure failure or when someone else surpasses them. When affection is tied to performance, even success feels insecure. The fear of losing approval becomes a heavy burden. What appears to be confidence may hide anxiety disguised as perfectionism.

Spiritually, this undermines the foundational truth of our identity in Christ. God does not define us by correlations. The worth He assigns to each soul remains constant, regardless of achievements or accolades. Each person's journey is uniquely guided by divine hands. When families distort this truth by promoting competition, they unintentionally prioritise accomplishments over character, visibility over humility, and favouritism over unconditional love.

The consequences of this distortion are significant. Adults who were once underappreciated cousins often carry silent shame. Some may strive for excessive success to regain lost validation, while others live quietly, convinced they lack the necessary qualities. In both situations, their identities are shaped not by grace but by a persistent shadow of contrasts.

Long-Term Emotional and Relational Impact

Jealousy among cousins often persists into adulthood. It re-emerges years later during family gatherings, the extent of life sharing, and the genuine feeling of being seen by relatives. As adults, they may no longer compete for attention, but many still feel the pain of never having received it.

These early comparisons can lead to strained relationships and estrangement. Some cousins choose to keep their distance to avoid the emotional discomfort of situations where they once felt inferior. Others maintain a façade of unity while secretly harbouring resentment. Occasionally, this competitive dynamic spills into the next generation, with the children of cousins becoming the new focus of it. The damage to relationships is profound. Bonds that could have been nurturing become shallow or strained. Trust is hard to build because the foundation lacks stability. Emotional wounds often go unspoken because, in many families, no culture of healing includes confrontation, confession, or restoration. Instead, silence and forced smiles conceal disappointment and rejection.

Without intentional change, these cycles continue. The cousin who felt "less than" may unconsciously overcorrect with their children, pushing them to compete or comparing them unfavourably to their relatives. Thus, the generational pattern continues.

Healing and Interventions

Healing these dynamics requires more than mere avoidance. When families understand that jealousy distorts their connections, they can begin to dismantle the labels that shape their identities and damage trust. One significant change is to redefine family gatherings as opportunities for sharing personal stories rather than providing status updates. Instead of assessing value based on jobs, degrees, or possessions, families can exchange tales of perseverance, forgiveness, and growth. A thoughtful gesture from an aunt or support from a cousin during tough times are the moments that restore dignity and remind each member that their worth isn't defined in relation to others.

Spiritual restoration involves rejecting the misconception that love must be competed for. The Gospel teaches that God's love is abundant, not limited. There is no need to outdo a cousin to feel chosen or valued. True maturity arises when we celebrate those we may have envied in the past, recognising that they have become the people we admire. When we find joy in others' achievements without feeling threatened, jealousy loses its power. Elders and parents play a pivotal role in shaping the family's emotional environment. Their words have a significant impact on how children perceive themselves.

Recognising every child for who they are, based on their inherent God-given value rather than distinctions to others, serves as a potent antidote to generational jealousy. A simple affirmation like "I'm proud of your unique qualities" can begin to heal years of internal pain.

Narrative reframing and family dialogue sessions can help uncover shared moments of unity that may have been forgotten. Cousins who once viewed each other as rivals might discover they share similar fears, pressures, or even admiration. Bringing these truths to light in a safe and affirming setting can help mend broken trust. If jealousy can weaken the bonds of a natural family, it can easily disrupt the connections within a spiritual family. Unlike cousins who may interact infrequently, believers often live and work closely with one another.

In the next chapter, we will discuss how jealousy manifests within the church. In this setting, roles are meant to serve rather than compete, and gifts should build up the community, not divide it. However, even in spiritual environments, the desire for recognition, favour, or anointing can create an atmosphere where envy distorts God's intended purpose.

In the body of Christ, as in a family, healing starts when we remember that love is not something we can earn. Favour is not a prize to be contested. In God's Kingdom, no one needs to outshine another to feel secure.

Jealousy in the Church

Churches, as sanctuaries, are where the transformative power of God's Spirit is at work, healing hearts and changing lives. However, in many congregations, these refuges have gradually turned into spaces of hidden competition and subtle displacement. What may seem like simple discomfort or emotional tension often masks something deeper: a spiritual force that undermines unity, disrespects God's sovereignty, and influences the community in subtle yet profound ways.

Jealousy within the body of Christ usually doesn't show up as outright hostility. It often enters quietly through competitions, hurt feelings, or feelings of inadequacy. When it remains unacknowledged or is labelled as 'normal,' it can become a gateway for more profound spiritual disruption. A personal struggle may evolve into a foothold for a spirit that seeks to obstruct the very movement of God we profess to desire. This deceptive nature of jealousy calls for caution and vigilance in our spiritual lives.

When God's Choice Feels Offending

In spiritually active communities, where individuals sincerely seek God and long for His presence, jealousy often arises and targets those God is using. Individuals who possess a unique grace or special spiritual calling may become the target of gossip, suspicion, or resistance.

Their rise can bring to light the feelings of others who may feel forgotten or underappreciated.

Those who have faithfully served for years may struggle when God elevates someone new, especially if that person is younger or from outside their familiar circle. It can be painful to be overlooked, particularly after dedicating time in the background. If this pain remains unhealed in God's presence, it can transform into a more harmful belief: that the other person does not deserve their position.

Once this belief takes root, jealousy often follows. Jealousy can easily infiltrate relationships, ministries, prayer groups, and even entire church structures. For instance, it can lead to power struggles among leaders, favouritism in ministry assignments, or gossip and backbiting among members. All these manifestations of jealousy are forms of opposing God's work.

Jealousy as a Spiritual Force

When jealousy goes unaddressed, it evolves into a spiritual stronghold, a term used to describe a deeply rooted and pervasive influence of the enemy in a person's life. In some ministry settings, intercessors and spiritual leaders recognise that jealousy can serve as a legal basis for the enemy to hinder or afflict individuals.

This agreement often does not come from the person being attacked; rather, it arises from those around them, individuals who judge their calling, resent their influence, or believe they do not deserve the platform God has given them.

Consequently, these individuals may face unusual resistance, sudden health problems, strained relationships, financial difficulties, or ministry obstacles. When prayers and fasting do not lead to breakthroughs, it becomes clear that deeper issues are at play. Only when jealousy is identified as the root, stemming from surrounding relationships, past environments, or even generational patterns, does the oppression begin to lift.

It is important to understand this principle: when someone agrees that another person's calling, blessing, or success is undeserved, they unknowingly align themselves with the voice of the accuser. The enemy seeks agreement to gain ground, using that internal judgment as permission to resist and torment. What may seem like a simple thought, such as "Why them?" or "They don't deserve it?", can evolve into a spiritual agreement that inflicts real harm. This dynamic explains why individuals in visible ministry roles often endure warfare that feels personal, extended, and inexplicable. The enemy exploits the jealousy of others as a tactic of attack. It is not solely the fault of the person being targeted; the actual battle occurs in the unseen agreements around them.

The Origin of Jealousy in Scripture

To grasp the seriousness of jealousy, we can refer back to its origin in scripture. The fall of Satan, as described in Isaiah 14 and Ezekiel 28, stemmed from his desire to rise above his appointed position and claim glory for himself. He was jealous, not only of God but also of humanity. Despite being adorned with beauty and fulfilling his heavenly assignment, he wanted more. This jealousy transformed into rebellion, and his desire to ascend ultimately led to his fall.

Today, that same spirit still lurks in churches, whispering lies and fostering comparisons. It tells leaders, "You're being replaced." It tells volunteers, "You're not important anymore." It tells believers, "They're taking your place." When these whispers are accepted as truth, jealousy infiltrates our hearts. The enemy is envious of God's people because of what we possess intimacy with God, the indwelling of the Spirit, the righteousness of Christ, and access to grace, things he has lost. Thus, his mission is straightforward: if he can't have it, he will try to ruin it for us. One of his most effective tactics is to stir up jealousy in others, turning blessings into points of contention.

Jealousy Among Leaders: Insecurity, Influence, and the Pulpit

Jealousy isn't confined to church members; it is especially prevalent among leaders. Pastors, elders, teachers, and ministry heads are highly vulnerable, particularly when success is measured by visibility, influence, or public affirmation.

Leaders may feel threatened when another minister rises quickly or gains a public platform. The temptation to compare is intensified by digital access. Livestreams, sermon clips, and social media can display one pastor's ministry to thousands, or even millions-of viewers. While some may find inspiration in this, others may feel overshadowed. In such situations, jealousy can masquerade as a doctrinal concern. A pastor might warn their congregation about a particular preacher, not due to theological issues, but because of personal discomfort. Sermons may begin to include warnings about "celebrity churches" or "social media preachers." What is often challenged is not the content of the messages, but rather their influence.

In some cases, pastors may prohibit their members from attending or listening to other ministries. While this can seem protective, it often conceals territorial insecurity. The aim becomes control rather than true discipleship. The pulpit can transform into a space where bitterness masquerades as boldness, and discernment is misread as fear.

When jealousy operates in this manner, it shapes the spiritual culture of the congregation. Members begin to reflect their leader's unarticulated resentment. They become suspicious of anything unfamiliar and confuse loyalty with isolation. The result is spiritual elitism, a belief that their church or leader is the only one God uses. This behaviour deeply grieves the Holy Spirit, who longs for unity across the body of Christ, not division.

Competition Across Platforms: Remote Rivalry in the Digital Church

The digital age has added a new dimension to jealousy within the church. Ministers and believers now have access to countless other voices at any time. This access can lead to feelings of being threatened by someone they have never met, simply because that person's video reached more viewers or their words received more attention.

This dynamic creates a form of "remote competition." A worship leader might envy another on the opposite coast, while a preacher may silently resent the ministry success of someone they only interact with online. Unbeknownst to them, their hearts may shift. They stop praying for God's movement in others and instead secretly hope that attention will return to them.

This lack of understanding often prompts criticism. Sometimes it emerges subtly, questioning someone's "methods" or "style." Other times, it escalates to bold accusations framed as spiritual concerns. Regardless of the form it takes, this behaviour breeds division.

What makes this situation particularly dangerous is that many individuals never address the root of their discomfort. They shy away from self-reflection, ultimately spreading doubt. This reluctance leads to widespread suspicion. Ministries start contending for relevance instead of working together for revival, causing the name of Jesus to be overshadowed by human ego.

Competing for Power: When Ministry Becomes a Battleground

Jealousy often goes beyond a desire for recognition; it frequently revolves around power and control. People compete not only for praise but also for authority. Ministry becomes politicised. Who gets to lead? Who has the final say? Who has direct access to the pastor? Who makes the key decisions?

This power struggle fosters an environment where spiritual maturity is confused with strategic manoeuvring. Individuals work behind the scenes to gain positions. Volunteers seek recognition, and team members subtly compete over who possesses more "spiritual gifts."

This phenomenon is widespread in leadership teams, worship departments, and other ministry groups. People might fast and pray, but their motives can be mixed. Testimonies become opportunities for self-promotion, intercession turns into a competition for revelations, and service feels like a performance. When power is at stake, individuals may fear losing it.This fear can prompt leaders to withhold opportunities from others, which leads to passive-aggressive behaviour, gossip, favouritism, and even spiritual manipulation. People may use scripture and prayer to disguise their desire for control. They focus more on defending their territory than fostering growth.

In the Kingdom of God, authority is not something to seize; it is a gift to be shared. When churches begin to reflect corporate hierarchies rather than embody a spiritual family, jealousy becomes the norm. As a result, the influence of the Holy Spirit is overshadowed by the struggle for power rooted in human desires.

Ministry Teams and the Silent Battle of Jealousy

The battle against jealousy is not confined to leadership positions. It can profoundly impact ministry teams, including those serving in children's ministry, ushering, worship, media, outreach, and small groups. These are often the environments where comparison thrives quietly.

Team members serve alongside each other week after week, observing who receives praise, who is chosen for specific tasks, and who gets promoted.

People might wonder why someone is asked to lead a song again or why they weren't acknowledged for their efforts. Others may find themselves comparing their spiritual gifts or level of visibility. Although these thoughts often remain unspoken, they can create a slow, bitter resentment. Over time, the joy of service can be overshadowed by this quiet discontent. When this atmosphere takes hold, individuals no longer serve out of love; they serve to prove their worth. Fasting may become a competition, and testimonies could turn into indirect contests.

Discernment can shift towards suspicion, and instead of building each other up, members may unknowingly tear one another down. Jealousy has the power to disrupt unity without loud conflict. It can lead people to withdraw emotionally, withhold encouragement, or wish for the failure of others. In such silence, negativity can thrive.

When Proximity Intensifies the Struggle

Typically, we do not envy those who are far removed from us; instead, we envy those closest to us, whose successes feel just within reach. This might be the person next to us in rehearsal or a co-leader on our team. Their blessings can sting because they remind us of what we feel we lack.

This explains why jealousy often spreads rapidly in local churches. It turns teammates into silent competitors and transforms the desire to serve into a need to be recognised. Over time, individuals may interpret someone else's promotion as a personal rejection. Eventually, they may no longer believe that God has a place for everyone. This belief can establish a fertile ground for jealousy to grow.

Recognising the Spiritual Infrastructure

When jealousy goes unconfessed, it becomes a spiritual agreement, a legal right that the enemy can exploit. People might think they're merely frustrated or ignored, but their resentment often empowers the very darkness they wish to avoid. Some ministers may encounter repeated setbacks without clear explanations. While they strive to walk uprightly, someone's unspoken agreement with negative influences opens doors in the spirit realm. Those harbouring jealousy become channels for spiritual resistance, while the individuals being envied carry an unexplained weight.

This issue extends beyond individuals; environments marked by jealousy can hold spiritual residue. Rooms where envy has been at work may begin to feel heavy. Children raised in homes characterised by comparison may carry that mind-set into adulthood. Unless these spiritual agreements are addressed, negative patterns can persist.

Cultivating Cultures of Honour

Healing must occur not only on an individual level but also on a cultural one. Churches should become places where success is celebrated, not feared. Leaders should model a spirit of celebration over competition, and team members ought to openly affirm one another. Honour must flow freely, from the platform to the parking lot. Teaching about jealousy should be an integral part of discipleship, offering not only warnings but also practical tools. People need to learn to recognise jealousy early, confess it, choose intercession over resentment, and trust God's sovereignty in deciding whom He uses and when.

Fixing Our Eyes on Christ

Ultimately, jealousy diminishes when Christ is at the centre of our focus. The more we concentrate on our positions, callings, or influence, the more threatened we may feel. However, when we exalt Christ above all else, we can rejoice regardless of through whom He chooses to work. John the Baptist expressed this perfectly: "He must increase, but I must decrease." This heart posture is what can heal the church. When Christ is glorified, everyone benefits. When the body of Christ embraces this truth, the spirit of jealousy loses its grip. While jealousy in the church often surfaces through roles, platforms, or power, its influence extends far beyond the sanctuary. Among believers, one of the most powerful, yet unspoken, triggers of jealousy is financial favour. As churches celebrate breakthroughs and testimonies, members might silently wonder, "Why not me?" As individuals serve and sacrifice, they may struggle with competing regarding jobs, homes, cars, and financial blessings. The issue of money is not solely practical; it is deeply spiritual. To undergo true healing from jealousy, we must confront its presence not only within ministry but also in our perceptions of provision, prosperity, and God's generosity.

PART FOUR: EXPOSING JEALOUSY'S DECEPTIVE CLOAK

From a Feeling to a Stronghold: How Jealousy Gains Ground

Most people see jealousy as an emotional response, often stemming from feelings of insecurity, neglect, or threat. For many, that's where the understanding ends. However, in spiritually discerning circles, particularly within deliverance and charismatic ministries, jealousy can signify more than a fleeting emotion. It isn't just something we feel; it can act through us. If left unaddressed, jealousy can evolve into a deep spiritual influence. What starts as a heart issue can grow strong enough to become a stronghold, even a spiritual presence that changes how a person thinks, speaks, and treats others.

This perspective is based on consistent spiritual insights recognised by believers through prayer, ministry, and discernment. The longer jealousy is left unaddressed, the more it becomes ingrained, distorting relationships, poisoning joy, and ultimately damaging the unity within the body of Christ. Jealousy often begins as an emotion, arising from feelings of being threatened by someone else's success, a loved one's affection, or a peer's position. However, others' stressed emotions do remain passive.

Scripture teaches that sin, when fully matured, leads to destruction; jealousy follows a similar path. Over time, individuals may react not only emotionally but also spiritually resistant toward the person they envy. They might avoid, criticise, gossip about, or distance themselves from that individual. These patterns are not random; in many deliverance settings, they are recognised as signs that a deeper spirit is at work, something beyond natural feelings propelling a person to act in ways they usually would not.

This is why spiritual discernment, the ability to perceive and understand spiritual realities, is essential. When a person wouldn't find themselves trapped in a cycle of resentment, bitterness, passive resistance, or an inexplicable dislike for someone who has done them no harm, it becomes vital to consider whether these feelings have moved beyond their soul and taken root in the spirit. Not every recurring thought originates solely in the mind; sometimes, spiritual doors have been opened.

In Numbers 5:14, the Old Testament mentions a "spirit of jealousy" in the context of a husband suspecting his wife of infidelity. While this doesn't explicitly mention a demon, the phrase helps understand jealousy as something more than a mere thought. It can settle within a person, stir suspicion, and provoke actions, whether right or wrong.

"For where you have envy and selfish ambition, there you find disorder and every evil practice." James 3:16 (NIV). This verse has become essential for many ministries focused on spiritual warfare. Jealousy does not stay passive; it opens the door to disorder. In biblical terms, spirits that cause disorder, confusion, or strife are never seen as originating from God. In spiritual terms, it can act like a counterfeit spirit, masquerading as godly caution or righteous concern while working to divide and distract. Consider a flourishing ministry team where one member's gift of hospitality makes newcomers feel welcome from the start. Members, those who once served on the greeting team, notice fewer smiles directed their way. Their desire to maintain order transforms into a covert effort to minimise the newcomer's influence: meetings are rescheduled so they cannot attend, newcomers revert to old channels, and scripture about humility is quoted repeatedly in ways that feel pointed rather than constructive.

Subtle Patterns That Fracture Community

Jealousy has a deceptive nature and often presents itself as truth. Jealousy is not a biblical virtue; order is essential. Jealousy aims to control situations for personal gain rather than to advance God's kingdom. To reveal this spirit, we need to align our actions with the fruits of the Spirit mentioned in Galatians 5:22-23, as described by God.

When we notice a lack of patience, kindness, and self-control and instead observe pride, division, or manipulation, we can identify the underlying spirit, not by its words, but by its consequences. Genuine spiritual authority enhances one's gifts, while jealousy restricts them. When jealousy appears as a spiritual influence, it dismisses reason and love. A person influenced by jealousy may react harshly, distort words, or create subtle divisions, often without realising their behaviour. Compliments directed toward others can be perceived as threats, disrupting group harmony. Instead of celebrating another's calling, the individual may exhibit irritation, defensiveness, or rivalry.

This behaviour tends to remain hidden, making it particularly insidious. Jealousy frequently disguises itself as concern, control, or false humility. In group settings, it can lead to isolation. The targeted individual may suddenly find themselves excluded from conversations, left out of invitations, or subtly stripped of influence. The group may remain unaware, yet the pattern is clear. This calls for a heightened sense of discernment and vigilance in our spiritual communities. This is especially common in ministry contexts. Teams that once prayed together may begin to drift apart. Once joyful worship bands can become distant, and leadership may become territorial. Friends who once valued each other may start to compete for influence and power.

This is not just a personal struggle, but a spiritual warfare that requires our immediate attention and action.

What makes this spirit particularly dangerous is its subtlety. It not only targets its victims but also corrupts the individuals who harbour it. Someone influenced by jealousy may believe they are upholding standards and preserving unity. However, beneath the surface, they might be hiding their fear of being overlooked or replaced. This underscores the crucial need for spiritual discernment in identifying and confronting jealousy.

When jealousy arises, it creates spiritual disorder and chaos. It is more than a fleeting emotion; it becomes a foothold for deceit and division.

Jealousy functions as a counterfeit spirit. It mimics traits that may seem righteous. It presents itself as caution but is rooted in fear; it appears as correction but is driven by competition. It pretends to be wise yet lacks true spiritual fruit. As Paul reminds us in Galatians 5:22-23, genuine spiritual fruit includes "love, joy, peace, patience", kindness, goodness, faithfulness, gentleness, and self-control." If our expressions of accountability, leadership, or discernment lack these qualities, we must question whether it is truly the Spirit of God or jealousy guiding us.

The counterfeit spirit

A counterfeit spirit mimics the qualities and language of God but originates from a different source. It may exhibit signs of wisdom, concern, and discernment, yet its effects include confusion, tension, control, and rivalry. Its purpose is not to protect but to possess. It does not affirm; it restricts. It does not love; it withholds. When permitted to persist, jealousy takes on a spiritual character, influencing decisions, communication, and leadership behaviour. It can attach itself to individuals, families, teams, friendships, creative spaces, professional environments, and ministry contexts. Wherever potential exists, jealousy works to limit and contain it.

In environments where this spirit prevails, it contradicts God's character. Instead of God's lying gifts, it hoards them. Rather than affirming identity, it undermines worth. Instead of celebrating differences, it enforces conformity. This behaviour can lead to atmospheres that are spiritually constrained, emotionally draining, and relationally unsafe, even when everyone seems to act appropriately. It is crucial to differentiate this counterfeit spirit from holy jealousy. The Bible describes God as a "jealous God" (Exodus 20:5), but His" jealousy arises from covenant love, not fear. He safeguards what belongs to Him, not from insecurity but because of His holiness.

Holy jealousy aligns with truth, while the counterfeit spirit seeks to possess what is not ours, stemming from a fear of losing relevance, love, or importance. Holy jealousy leads to righteousness, while counterfeit jealousy results in control. To confront this spirit, we must begin by examining ourselves and asking:

- Am I uncomfortable when others succeed?
- Do I struggle to affirm others without diminishing them?
- Have I used spiritual language to mask my insecurity?

When jealousy is brought to light, its power diminishes. However, it cannot be softened or negotiated; it must be renounced as a spiritual stronghold. This involves identifying it, rejecting its lies, and choosing truth in both thought and action. We need to declare: "This is not discernment. This is not love. This is jealousy, and it does not belong in my heart."

Next, we must actively choose to bless those from whom we previously withdrew. We should pray for those we once compared ourselves to serve rather than compete, affirm what we once viewed with suspicion, and thank God for the diverse ways He reveals His glory through others. Genuine spiritual authority empowers rather than suppresses. True love creates space, and authentic humility celebrates the achievements of others.

The Spirit of God rejoices in the success of others without feeling diminished.

Spiritual warfare is often not visible. It frequently hides within patterns. The spirit of jealousy does not announce itself through clear signs or abrupt changes. Instead, it infiltrates environments through subtle cues, emotional reactions, and repeated behaviours that create an atmosphere of resistance. To uncover this spirit, we must attune ourselves to what lies beneath the surface, how people react, what they avoid, and how the atmosphere shifts when specific individuals are mentioned or celebrated.

PART FIVE: FREEDOM AND RESTORATION

Unholy Contracts & Spiritual Alliances

Before we can find lasting freedom, we must dismantle the hidden spiritual agreements known as "unholy contracts" that allow jealousy to take root in our hearts. These contracts consist of silent vows we whisper in moments of pain, or pride, such as: "I will never let anyone outdo" me," "I refuse to be overlooked," or "I must prove my worth." "Even when these declarations" are spoken only in thought, they create spiritual footholds that invite jealousy to dwell within us. To break their power, we need to bring these agreements into the light and renounce them aloud:

"In the name of Jesus, I cancel every vow made out of fear, pride, or anxiety. I place these contracts under the blood of Christ and declare them null and void."

By severing the legal grounds that allow jealousy to thrive, we pave the way for genuine healing. This act of breaking these inner agreements empowers us to follow a five-step pathway toward restoration. First, we must confess aloud that envy has taken hold of us, admitting, "This is not from God. I need help."

This confession brings a sense of relief, acknowledging the grip of jealousy and opening us to receive divine mercy.

Next comes true repentance, turning away from the pride, fear, or rejection that laid the groundwork for jealousy. Repentance surpasses mere regret; it involves intentionally reorienting our hearts toward humility and reliance on God's goodness. After repentance, we renounce any remaining ties to scarcity thinking by declaring that there is more than enough space for every blessing to flourish. This act of renunciation brings a sense of freedom, as we reject thoughts that assert, "There's not enough for me," or "I must come "There must be recognition." In this act, we reclaim our identity as beloved children of God, turning away from the lies that once held us captive.

Then, we step into prayerful authority, commanding the spirit of jealousy to depart in Jesus' name. We do not negotiate or compromise; we remove any presence that contradicts the peace and unity the spirit of God brings. Finally, we replace the lies planted by jealousy with the truth of scripture. We declare that God shows no favouritism and that His gifts and callings are irrevocable. We affirm that He who began a good work in us will be faithful to complete it, and that as the Good Shepherd, He provides everything we need.

These declarations are not mere affirmations; they are spiritual tools that uproot the roots of envy and renew our minds in alignment with God's perspective. However, this five-step process is just the beginning of restoration. Many of the patterns that fuelled our jealousy likely did not begin in our own situations but may have been inherited from previous generations. In families where affection was given based on performance, we learned to equate love with achievement.

In families where siblings are compared and set against each other, we often internalise the belief that one person's success means another's failure. However, this is not always the case. For instance, a sibling's success can inspire and motivate others to strive for their own achievements. It is crucial to interrupt these generational patterns. We must present these inherited beliefs to God, confessing any idea that love must be earned or that one person's achievements diminish another's worth. Additionally, we should forgive those who passed down these harmful lies. By offering forgiveness, we invite the Holy Spirit to reshape our family narrative with grace and truth.

Once we address these patterns, we can create new rhythms of celebration and sincere affirmation in our relationships. We must focus on speaking words of life. We can honour others without measuring their success against our own and choose to bless rather than withhold.

Through these new practices, the next generation will see a different model, one where love is unconditional, calling is validated, and unity flourishes.

To maintain our freedom and prevent jealousy from creeping back in, we must diligently close every door that once allowed it in. Past wounds from unhealed offences and painful rejections provide fertile ground for envy to grow. When we hold onto grudges, we leave the door open for resentment to enter again. Insecurity about our worth can also create openings for envy, as can unchecked pride that convinces us we deserve more than others. What may start as a simple observation can turn into a relentless critic if left unchecked?

Closing these doors requires daily effort: offering forgiveness to those who have injured us, grounding our identity in Christ's love rather than seeking validation from others, and embracing a humble attitude that celebrates others without elevating ourselves.

Daily spiritual practices serve as our ongoing defence. We fill our minds with scripture, reflect on God's verses that reveal the emptiness of scarcity thinking and affirm God's abundant provision. We cultivate gratitude by internally acknowledging His blessings, training our hearts to recognise God's goodness instead of comparing our lives to others.

We also practice honour by genuinely affirming those around us, choosing to bless rather than compete. We commit to consistent prayer to remain connected to our source of strength, and when led, we engage in fasting to quiet our desires and heighten our spiritual awareness.

As we follow these rhythms, true peace takes hold. We find joy in the success of others because we recognise that their achievements do not diminish our worth in Christ. Relationships begin to heal as walls of suspicion crumble. Ministries and teams that once felt tense and divided come alive with purpose and unity. Families breathe easily as each member is recognised and celebrated for their unique gifts.

This peace is deep and genuine; it is the result of God's Spirit filling God's heart free of envy and full of truth. It is the assurance that, as children of a generous Father, we lack nothing and share an eternal inheritance that cannot fade. When deep joy replaces jealousy, our lives become testimonies of freedom, narratives that attract others to the One who can heal hearts and restore communities.

Ultimately, restoration is not just the absence of competition but the presence of a kind and loving approach that reflects God's kingdom. As we continue in repentance, prayer, scripture reading, God's gratitude, and honouring others, the spirit of jealousy finds no resting place within us.

Our narratives, once marked by envy and conflict, transform into stories of grace, unity, and abundance. This is the restoration God envisions, a life free from past burdens, empowered to celebrate every expression of His glory in us and in others glory in ourselves and others.

Prayer for Repentance, Forgiveness, and Victory over Jealousy

Dear Heavenly Father,

In this moment of humility, I come before you, laying bare my soul and seeking your divine guidance and forgiveness. I confess, O Lord, the burden of jealousy that weighs heavy upon my heart, clouding my vision and dimming the light of your love within me.

With a spirit of repentance, I turn to your word, finding solace and strength in the promises of your grace and mercy. As I meditate on your holy scriptures, may your words not just touch, but transform my heart and renew my spirit.

In Psalms 51:10, *I find the prayer of King David, a plea for cleansing and renewal: "Create in me a clean heart, O God, and renew a steadfast spirit within me." Like David, I humbly ask for your divine intervention, purifying me from the stain of jealousy and restoring within me a spirit of righteousness and peace.*

Grant me the courage to repent of my envy, O Lord, and the strength to turn away from thoughts and actions that dishonour you. Help me to embrace your forgiveness with gratitude and humility, knowing that your love surpasses all understanding and has the power to transform my heart and soul.

In Your word, I find the promise of victory over the power of darkness. In 1 John 4:4, you declare, "Greater is He who is in you than he who is in the world." With this truth as my shield and strength, I stand firm against the schemes of the enemy, confident in your power to overcome every obstacle.

As I walk in the light of your truth, may your love cast out all fear and insecurity, replacing them with confidence and peace. Your grace empowers me to love others as you have loved me, rejoicing in their blessings and celebrating their successes without envy or resentment, knowing that your love is my strength and shield.

Heavenly Father, I willingly surrender my heart to you, trusting in your unfailing love and mercy. Guide me along the path of righteousness, which I may walk in your ways and bring glory to your holy name.

In the name of Your Son, Jesus Christ, I pray. Amen

A JOURNALING GUIDE

JOURNEY TO OVERCOMING JEALOUSY

Introduction to Journaling

Welcome to this intentional and healing space a guide designed to help you grow through the lens of journaling and confront the challenges of jealousy. While jealousy can cloud perspective and affect emotional well-being, journaling becomes a practical and empowering way to gain clarity and take control of your inner world.

In life's unfolding story, each of us is the main character. At times, jealousy emerges as a quiet adversary, challenging our sense of peace and self-worth often stirred by comparison or deep-rooted insecurity. Yet within this struggle lies an invitation to understand yourself more deeply. A journal becomes your personal sanctuary, a place to observe, process, and transform. It offers room to explore your emotions, challenge limiting beliefs, and cultivate a mind-set grounded in confidence and contentment.

This practice supports growth in many ways. It helps you articulate emotions; notice thought patterns and express yourself freely. Through simple tools like gratitude entries, setting personal goals, and affirmations rooted in truth, you'll gradually shift from emotional turmoil to inner resilience.

More than anything, this guide is a companion. Let it walk with you as you learn to recognise triggers, realign your focus, and embrace the strength already within you. One entry at a time, you're building a healthier, more self-aware life.

Exploring Jealousy

Reflection Prompts:

Identify Triggers: Reflect on specific situations that evoke feelings of jealousy. Is it related to comparison, recognition, relationships, or unmet expectations?

Explore the Root Emotions: Are these feelings tied to insecurity, fear of inadequacy, or a need for validation? Describe how these emotions manifest in your thoughts and behavior.

Relational Impact: Consider how jealousy affects your relationships with others and with yourself. Does it lead to distance, resentment, or inner conflict? In what ways does it influence your self-esteem and emotional stability?

Open Reflection: Use your journal to explore your experiences with jealousy. Write freely and without judgment. Capture your thoughts, emotions, and any insights that surface. This is your opportunity to gain clarity, perspective, and a deeper understanding of your heart.

By delving into the depths of jealousy, you'll uncover valuable insights into your emotional world and relationships paving the way for personal healing and growth

Forgiveness and Letting Go

Reflection Prompts:

Acknowledge the Impact: Reflect on a time when jealousy negatively affected your relationships or your well-being. What emotions and triggers were at play?

***Understand the Cost*:** How has holding onto jealousy, comparison, or resentment impacted your peace, joy, or emotional health?

Receiving Jealousy from Others: Have you ever been the target of someone else's jealousy? How did it affect you? What did you learn from that experience?

***Define Forgiveness**:* What does forgiveness mean to you in the context of jealousy? How can releasing others and yourself free you emotionally and spiritually?

***Name the Barriers**:* Are there specific fears, beliefs, or wounds keeping you from forgiving yourself or others? What would it take to begin letting go?

Journaling Exercises:

Letter of Release: Write a letter to someone you need to forgive (you don't have to send it). Be honest. Acknowledge the hurt but also express your decision to release the weight of resentment and move forward in freedom.

Self-Forgiveness & Compassion: If you struggle with guilt or shame, journal affirmations of grace. For example: "I forgive myself for past mistakes. I choose healing over self-judgment."

Gratitude Through Forgiveness: Write down the unexpected gifts that came from difficult experiences lessons learned, deeper empathy, stronger boundaries, or increased wisdom.

Act of Kindness: Engage in a small act of kindness as a symbol of release. It could be toward yourself or someone else. Let this be a physical representation of your decision to move forward.

"Forgiveness isn't about excusing the pain; it's about choosing freedom over bitterness. By releasing others, you release yourself."

Practicing Self-Compassion

When healing from jealousy or comparison, it's easy to be harsh with yourself. But true transformation comes when you meet your imperfections with kindness. This section helps you shift from self-criticism to self-compassion.

Journaling Activities & Prompts:

Gratitude for Self: Create a list of things you genuinely appreciate about yourself, your strengths, efforts, small victories, and character traits. This helps you see your own worth more clearly.

"I am thankful for how I always try again, even
when it's hard."

Self-Compassion Space: Use a few pages in your journal as a safe space to process moments of failure, insecurity, or regret without judgment. Respond to those moments with grace, as you would to a close friend.

Prompt: "Write about a time you were too
hard on yourself. What would a kinder version
of you say in that moment?"

Self-Care Mapping: Make a list of self-care practices that nourish your mind, body, and soul.

Include things that ground you, such as prayer, music, nature, laughter, or quality time with loved ones.

Prompt: "What does true rest look like for me?"

Exploring the Inner Critic: Reflect on the voice of your inner critic. What does it often say? Where might those beliefs come from? How do they affect your decisions and confidence?

Prompt: *"Is this voice true? Kind? Helpful? If not, what would a more compassionate voice say instead?"*

Nurturing Self-Talk: Develop affirmations or phrases that reinforce your worth and shift your mindset when you feel discouraged or not enough.

Example:
"I am growing, and that is enough."

Progress Over Perfection: Jealousy often thrives in a perfectionist mindset. Use your journal to celebrate progress, no matter how small. Track how you're evolving, not just how you're performing.

Prompt: "What did I handle better today than I would have a year ago?"

Self-compassion isn't self-indulgence, it's spiritual maturity. It's choosing love where shame once lived."

Cultivating Self-Esteem

Jealousy often has roots in low self-worth or uncertainty about our value. Cultivating healthy self-esteem empowers you to celebrate others without feeling threatened and to affirm your own unique calling.

Reflection Prompts:

Strengths and Talents:

What are some qualities, skills, or talents you admire in yourself?

How have they shaped your personal or professional journey?

Overcoming Challenges:

Think back on a difficult season or moment you've overcome.

What inner strengths helped you endure? What did you learn?

Core Values:

What do you stand for?

What values guide your decisions, relationships, and life choices?

Personal Integrity:

Are you living in alignment with who you are?

Where do your actions and identity feel connected or disconnected?

Journaling Exercises:

Strengths Inventory: Create a list of your top character strengths, things like courage, creativity, empathy, discipline, or determination. Note real-life examples where these qualities have been visible. *Prompt:* "When have I felt most like myself? What was I doing, and who was I becoming?"

Affirming Self-Talk: Write affirmations that reinforce your God-given value. Use them to rewire limiting beliefs and build a healthier internal dialogue.

Examples:
"I am enough because I was created with purpose."

"My worth is not based on what I achieve, but on who I am."

Rewriting the Narrative: Identify a self-limiting belief (e.g., "I'm not as good as they are"). Then rewrite it into an empowering truth (e.g., "I bring something uniquely valuable to the table.").

Setting Goals for Growth

Once you've begun healing from jealousy and strengthening your self-worth, the next step is to intentionally grow. Setting clear, faith-aligned goals empowers you to move forward with purpose and direction.

Goal-Setting Guidance:
Use the SMART Method - Ensure your goals are:

Specific – What exactly do you want to achieve?
Measurable – How will you track progress?
Achievable – Is it realistic for where you are?
Relevant – Does it align with your values and life vision?
Time-bound – What's your timeline or checkpoint?

Balance Short & Long-Term Goals
Set goals that offer both immediate encouragement and long-term transformation. Small wins build confidence for bigger ones.

Reflection Prompts:

"What areas of my life do I desire to see growth in emotionally, spiritually, relationally, or professionally?"

"What goals feel aligned with my identity and calling?"

"How will achieving this goal contribute to my sense of purpose or peace?"

"What step can I take this week to move toward this goal?"

"What obstacles might arise, and how can I prepare for them in faith and wisdom?"

"Goal setting is more than productivity, it's intentional living. As you commit your plans to God, trust that He will direct your steps (Proverbs 16:3)."

Affirmations for Confidence

Affirmations help rewire negative thinking and reinforce a God-given identity. When rooted in truth, they combat insecurity, strengthen faith, and empower you to walk confidently, even in areas where jealousy once ruled.

How to Create Faith-Based Affirmations:

Make Them Personal

Use "I" statements grounded in truth (e.g., "I am chosen, equipped, and empowered by God.")

Speak to the Root

Target areas where jealousy or fear tends to show up, such as comparison, rejection, or unworthiness.

Ground Them in Scripture

Use God's Word to anchor your affirmations in truth that transcends emotion.

Reflection Prompts:

"Where do I most often feel insecure or doubtful?"

"What truth from God's Word speaks directly to that insecurity?"

"What would I say to encourage a friend in the same situation?"

Examples of Affirmations (Rooted in Scripture):
"I can do all things through Christ who strengthens me." – Philippians 4:13

A reminder that God's strength empowers every challenge you face.

"*God has not given me a spirit of fear, but of power, love, and a sound min*d." – 2 Timothy 1:7

You are not helpless or broken, you are equipped by the Spirit of God.

Incorporation Ideas:

Speak them aloud during morning devotionals or while journaling.

Write them on sticky notes or cards and place them where you'll see them often.

Create a "Confidence Page" in your journal filled with your favourite affirmations.

"Confidence built on truth endures. Let your affirmations remind you of who you are and whose you are."

Reflecting on Scripture

God's Word offers clarity, comfort, and correction when navigating difficult emotions like jealousy. This section invites you to reflect deeply on scriptures that speak to envy, forgiveness, and spiritual growth helping you realign your heart with God's truth.

Scripture Selections & Journaling Prompts

On Jealousy

Proverbs 14:30
"A heart at peace gives life to the body, but envy rots the bones."

James 3:16
"For where you have envy and selfish ambition, there you find disorder and every evil practice."

Reflection Prompts:

How have these verses helped me understand the deeper damage of jealousy?

In what ways is peace of heart more life-giving than striving or comparison?

What does "a heart at peace" look like in my current season?

On Forgiveness

Ephesians 4:32
"Be kind and compassionate to one another, forgiving each other, just as in Christ God forgave you."

Colossians 3:13
"Bear with each other and forgive one another... Forgive as the Lord forgave you."

Reflection Prompts:

Who do I still need to forgive and why is that hard for me?

How does knowing I'm already forgiven shape my ability to extend grace to others?

What would forgiveness look like in action for me this week?

On Growth and Transformation

Philippians 3:13–14
"Forgetting what is behind and straining toward what is ahead, I press on…"

Romans 12:2
"Be transformed by the renewing of your mind…"

Reflection Prompts:

What old beliefs or habits do I need to leave behind in this journey?

How is God inviting me to grow in this season?

What is one mindset I want to renew with truth?

Integration & Application

How can I apply these scriptures practically in my daily life?

What verse speaks most directly to my heart right now, and why?

How can I incorporate these truths into my affirmations, prayers, or responses to others?

The Word of God doesn't just inform, it transforms. Let these scriptures guide your healing, correct your vision, and call you into freedom."

Daily Gratitude Journal

Gratitude is a powerful antidote to jealousy. It shifts your focus from what you lack to what you already have. A consistent gratitude practice rewires your heart to see abundance, not scarcity and prepares you to celebrate others without feeling diminished.

Daily Practice Instructions

Start Your Day with Intention: Set aside a few quiet moments each morning to reflect and journal before the day begins.

List 3 Things You're Grateful For: These can be small or big: the kindness of a friend, a moment of peace, answered prayer, progress in your healing, or simply a warm cup of tea.

Be Honest and Specific: You can write full reflections or just short notes; whatever helps you express true appreciation.

Let Gratitude Flow Freely: Don't overthink it. Your journal is a safe space. Express what feels real, whether it's a beautiful sunrise, a scripture that moved you, or a personal breakthrough.

Example Prompts:
"Today, I'm thankful for..."
"One thing I overlooked but appreciate now is..."
"Someone I'm grateful for and why..."
"A recent moment of joy or peace was..."

When you start your day with gratitude, you train your heart to look for blessings instead of burdens. Over time, contentment grows and jealousy fades."

Tracking Progress

Healing is not linear but it is measurable. Documenting your progress allows you to see how far you've come, recognise patterns, celebrate victories, and approach setbacks with grace rather than guilt. This section is about building awareness and resilience.

Journaling Successes

Use these prompts to acknowledge how you're growing in your response to jealousy:

Describe a recent situation where you managed jealousy with maturity. What did you do differently, and how did it feel?

Reflect on a time when you chose trust, contentment, or love instead of comparison. What was the result?

List 3 specific wins, small or big that show evidence of your emotional growth.

Reflecting on Setbacks

Setbacks don't mean failure. They are moments for reflection and redirection.

Describe a time recently when jealousy resurfaced. What triggered it, and how did you respond?

Are there recurring thoughts or scenarios that still challenge you? What truth can you speak to those situations?

What would grace look like for yourself in this moment?

Lessons Learned

Growth isn't just about getting it right; it's about learning from it all.

What have I discovered about myself or my relationships through this journey?
What belief has shifted that now brings me more freedom or peace?

List 3 key takeaways that will help guide your future decisions and interactions.

Action Steps Moving Forward

Reflect on how you've changed since starting this guide. Where have you grown? What areas still need attention?

Set 1 goal for the week ahead related to your continued healing.

(e.g., "This week, I will pause when comparison hits and write a truth-based affirmation instead.")
Write a final affirmation to anchor your commitment: "I am no longer ruled by jealousy. I choose peace, purpose, and growth."

Progress is not about perfection; it's about persistence. Keep showing up, one honest entry at a time."

Final Thoughts

You've taken brave and intentional steps toward healing. Confronting jealousy isn't easy, it asks you to look inward with honesty, extend forgiveness, build resilience, and embrace your God-given identity. But you've done it. One entry at a time, you've chosen transformation.

This journaling guide was designed to walk with you, not as a quick fix, but as a companion on a longer journey of self-discovery and spiritual maturity.

Overcoming jealousy doesn't happen in one moment it unfolds through continuous self-awareness and a willingness to grow. Give yourself time and grace. Every moment of reflection is a victory.

Your journal isn't just paper; it's a reflection of your journey, your healing, and your prayers. Keep using it as a space to dream, release, express, and realign. Some days you'll feel empowered. Other days may be harder. That's okay. Celebrate growth when it comes and show yourself kindness when you stumble. You are not failing, you are evolving.

Through every part of this process, pain, reflection, forgiveness, growth, and God's grace have been present. Let His love continues to guide you as you walk forward into a life of peace, trust, and freedom.

> You are not defined by your jealousy. You are defined by the truth of who God says you are, chosen, loved, enough, and free.

With warmest wishes for your continued growth, healing, and fulfilment.

By God's grace, you've begun. Now keep going.

ABOUT THE AUTHOR

Seetse Masigo is a dedicated writer committed to helping individuals discover their true selves. She ministers across cultural and background boundaries with grace and clarity and is well known for her profound insights and anointing to speak into the innermost places of the heart.

Her work gently guides people toward healing, purpose, and freedom by revealing the spiritual and emotional patterns that hold them back through Scripture and storytelling.

She is committed to helping readers live unapologetically in the fullness of their God-given calling and restoring wholeness. Her first book, Not Jealous, was written with conviction, consideration, and a desire to see people's lives changed from the inside out.

www.ingramcontent.com/pod-product-compliance
Lightning Source LLC
LaVergne TN
LVHW011245080426
835509LV00005B/638

9780796186775